# Trauma and Tea

Essays on Trauma, Recovery and
Growing up the Hard Way

**Matthew Heneghan**

BIG FLAG
PRESS

Big Flag Press

# Also By

**A Medic's Mind**

A memoir of trauma, addiction, and recovery

**Woven in War**

Stories of service, sacrifice, and the echoes of conflict

**Trauma and Tea**

*Essays on Trauma, Recovery, and Growing Up the Hard Way*

---

**Awards & Contributions**

Two-time winner – Word on the Lake Writers' Festival

CBC Freelance Contributor

# CONTENTS

Book Cover by Big Flag Press

First edition 2026

ISBN: 978-1-7776492-1-0

# Author's Note

The stories contained within this book are drawn from real-life experiences and events. They reflect personal memories, professional encounters, and emotional truths. In the interest of privacy, safety, and legal integrity, certain names, dates, locations, and identifying details have been altered or omitted. While the heart of each story remains intact, any resemblance to actual individuals—living or deceased—is either purely coincidental or used with permission.

This work is not intended to serve as medical advice, nor does it reflect the views of any past employers, agencies, or organizations.

# About the Author

Matthew Heneghan is a former Canadian Armed Forces member and paramedic who spent nearly two decades running toward the kinds of moments most people spend their lives avoiding. Born in England and raised in British Columbia, he built a life on service, survival, and storytelling long before he ever called himself a writer.

After years on the front lines—first in uniform, then in addiction, grief, PTSD, and recovery—Matthew turned to writing not as a hobby, but as a way to stay alive. What began as personal reflection evolved into a voice readers connected with for its honesty, gallows humour, and refusal to hide the messier parts of being human.

He is the author of *A Medic's Mind*, an award-winning memoir that resonated across first responder, veteran, and mental health communities. His work has appeared on CBC and through his long-running podcast, *Unwritten Chapters – Life After Trauma*, where he speaks candidly about trauma, healing, and the absurdity stitched between the two.

Matthew lives in British Columbia with his wife, Sheena, and their beautiful blended family. When he's not writing, he's likely drinking tea, reading a book, walking the hilly roads of his hometown, or roaming backroads with the same childhood best friend who appears throughout his stories. He also helps build community projects like The Haunting of Falkland, an annual Halloween event run by a small but dedicated group of volunteers to raise money for local first responders and other community fixtures.

He does not write to impress the world. He writes to tell the truth of it—and to make sure the people who've been through hell know they're not the only ones who made the trip.

To my dearest wife, Sheena — your love inspires my happiness, and that happiness inspired this book.

And to my brother, Drew — without you, growing up would have been impossible. Thank you for the memories and for the love we still share today.

# INTRODUCTION

My name is Matthew Heneghan. (I typically follow that with: and I'm and alcoholic), but, hang on... we'll get to that.

I've been a soldier. A paramedic. An addict. A patient. A husband. A man on the edge. A man bathed in hope. A writer. An asshole.

...You know, I could keep going on with colourful adjectives, but I think you get the idea. A flawed man with, at times, the best of intentions.

I've held the hands of the dying and the forgotten. I've driven home in a uniform soaked with the blood of strangers. I've shaken through detox and sat across from therapists who gently helped me unearth things I'd long since buried. And I've found, somehow, the will to keep going.

I didn't grow up with much. Trauma came early and stayed late. I joined the military thinking I might outrun it while doing some good in the world. Then I became a paramedic, hoping maybe I could save others in ways that I too was saved. For a while, that purpose kept me afloat.

Until it didn't.

Waves generally weigh more than coping mechanisms.

Eventually, the weight of all that I'd witnessed—and all that I hadn't dealt with — caught up with me. It looked a lot like PTSD. It was PTSD. A diagnosis that would find me in 2017. And addiction. And loneliness disguised as anger. But this isn't just a story about what's broken. It's also about what's still working. About healing. About clawing toward hope even when your hands are bloody and your fingernails are chipped jagged. When hope is so far away it exists only as a myth, or something for other people.

This book isn't written in a straight line, because my life hasn't been one.

Christ, are any of our lives?

These are essays, fragments, and reflections. Pieces of a life built in the aftermath. Some are gritty. Some are soft. All of them are true.

I have lived a remarkable life. Bruises and all. I've met a lot of amazing people along the way. People I will introduce you to through story.

If you're here, reading this — thank you.

I hope you find something in these pages that makes you feel a little less alone. Because we are never quite as alone as we may feel.

I promise.

— Matthew Heneghan

"You never know the value of a moment until it has become memory."

— Unknown

# Simpler Times
# (...Kind of)

# Sunburnt Memories and a Shopping Cart Named Carty

For a guy who spent most of his life resenting the sun, I sure found myself smiling under it this morning.

It was 08:45, and there I was, barefoot in my backyard, tea in hand, already sweating through a shirt I didn't want to wear. The heat hung heavy, the kind of oppressive humidity that usually reminds me of death, not joy. But damned if I didn't feel a smile teasing its way onto my face.

Blame Drew.

He's my best friend, my brother from another mother. We met in grade six and immediately became inseparable little punks — one long, uninterrupted streak of adolescent misdemeanors and snack breaks. As adults, we live close, but adulthood does what adulthood does — pulls you apart with calendars, kids, careers, and the crushing obligation of "being responsible."

Lately though, life's let up. We've found time to reconnect. Mini road trips, slow drives through mountains, lakeside stops, aimless detours through the desert like two middle-aged delinquents chasing ghosts. But this morning's smile wasn't about all that.

It was about a shopping cart.

There was a summer: one of those scorched-earth ones, the kind where the horizon wobbles and time feels like it's melting, where Drew and I, age fourteen and full of hell, were loitering around town. We'd already hit the corner store for slushies and sugar-coated regret, but boredom still gnawed at us. So, we did what dumb kids do: wandered.

We talked about all the essentials: wrestling, hockey, girls, girls who liked hockey, and what we'd say to girls if we ever found our balls long enough to say it.

Eventually, we ended up at the wharf — again. By now the sun was merciless, the sky a blank blue slab with no shade in sight. As we ambled along the trails near the water, something glittered off to the side like a secret. Curiosity, that great teenage engine, pulled us toward it.

A shopping cart. Rusted, abandoned, half-swallowed by weeds and reckless abandon. A relic far from its natural grocery store habitat. Drew and I looked at each other with that unspoken telepathy only found in best friends and war veterans.

You already know what happened next.

We pulled the cart free from nature's grip. It wobbled like hell, especially the front wheel, which had all the coordination of a drunk toddler, but it rolled. And that's all we needed.

"Let's take it through the Timmies drive-thru," I said, completely serious.

Drew didn't even blink. Of course he didn't. That kid would follow me into a fire even if it meant his end.

I pushed. He climbed in. It was glorious. It was stupid. It was everything.

Then, halfway to our caffeine-fueled finish line, it hit me — we didn't sound like a car. We needed engine noise, or the drive-thru lady would toss us out like expired Timbits.

Drew solved that with his mouth. Literally. He started making truck sounds — wet, salivatory, ridiculous sounds — and I laughed so hard I nearly sent us into a ditch. But I had a better idea.

We raced back to my place. I grabbed my old boombox, a blank cassette, and a mic. We stood outside, recording the rumble of passing trucks like we were producing the next Pearl Jam album. Pure genius.

We loaded the boombox into the cart, rewound the tape, hit play and returned to the scene of our dumbassery.

We got through the drive-thru.

We ordered. We paid. The lady opened the window and was greeted by a grinning kid in a shopping cart and another one pushing him, a static-laced engine hum pouring from our mobile jukebox like some poor man's Fast & Furious parody. Vin would be embarrassed.

She gave us the drinks. Reluctantly. Confused. Probably reconsidering her career choices.

We rode off into the blazing day with Ice Caps in hand, our cart, our music, and the kind of pride you can only feel after getting away with something you probably shouldn't have tried in the first place.

We ended up back at the wharf. Same sun. Same bench. Same friendship. And we laughed like idiots. I remember tapping the side of the cart, whispering, "Atta girl, Carty... atta girl."

That's what had me smiling today. That memory. That sun. That stupid, beautiful day.

Time passes. The summers stretch on. The tragedies pile up. Some days the sun still reminds me of blood, of heatstroke calls, of bodies in alleyways and the ones we couldn't save.

But other days, like this morning, it reminds me of Drew, of slushies and stolen carts and adolescent invincibility. And that, I can live with.

With all that finally confessed, if you're reading this, take my advice: let the sun in. Not all the way. Not recklessly. Just enough.

Enough to remember what was good. Enough to know you're still here. Enough to make you smile at 08:45 in your backyard while sipping tea and thinking about your best friend steering a deathtrap into a bush like it was a goddamn Olympic event.

Enjoy the rest of your summer.

# The Shit We Keep in Lockers

Childhood is a funny thing for me to muse on. And I don't mean funny ha-ha. I mean funny like an old bruise you forgot was there until someone presses on it. I read somewhere that comedy is just tragedy plus time. If that's true, then boyhood was a goddamn laugh factory.

I had the usual growing pains: hormones, insecurity, the occasional pimple. But I also played through all that with a home team that was falling apart. My mother was an addict. My father? Absent. Actually incarcerated — which is basically absentee parenting with a jumpsuit and cell block.

By the time I was nine or ten, mom got the kind of cancer you don't walk away from clean. She beat the disease, but not the cure. That whole ordeal introduced her to painkillers, which introduced her to sleep aids, which introduced me to watching my mother drool on herself while holding a cigarette like it might hold all the answers.

That's the kind of shit that sticks. That's the kind of shit that makes you question whether tragedy plus time really equals a punchline, or just solemnity with a different name.

Fast forward to the other day. I was standing in the kitchen, sipping tea like the aging cliché I've become, when I saw Claire. My stepdaughter — though I hate that term — putting the finishing touches on some cosplay outfit for Comicon. She and her friend were buzzing with excitement, this vibrant hum that filled the house and echoed through every inch of my chest. And just like that, I was gone. Swallowed by steam, falling into a warm pocket of memory. The kind that grabs you by the collar and takes you back to a version of yourself you barely remember anymore.

I was six when I moved from England. Skinny, awkward, and legally blind. Coke-bottle glasses. Average looks... if you're being generous. You'd think that would've helped me blend in. It didn't. In fact, it made me a bullseye for the Neanderthals of the hallway. Chief among them: Neil Pritchard. Guy used to flick my glasses off my face like it was his God-given right. One time he chipped the lens and I had this damn glint in my eye for months every time the sun came out. I never told my mom. She'd just have blamed me anyway.

And now I'm in my forties. Jesus Christ, that comes fast.

I've got a wife; she has two amazing kids — Claire and Olivia — and a best friend named Drew. Same Drew I met in sixth grade.

Still around.

Still my person.

It was a memory of him that really set me off that day. We were in eighth grade, at J.L. Jackson School in Salmon Arm: a charming little penitentiary for children. It was spring. The kind of afternoon that whispers promise of summer. We were standing behind the lockers, number 214, burned into memory like a scar that healed funny, when Drew said, "You gotta see this."

Behind that dented old locker was a hole. Not a crack. Not a gap. A goddamn passageway. A secret tunnel into the school's underbelly. The kind of thing that felt like it belonged in The Goonies or Stand by Me. Which meant, of course, we had to go in.

So, we did. No questions. Just instinct and zeal.

It smelled like dust and time. Like old paper and forgotten maps freshly unearthed. There were old desks, typewriters, carved initials. History, just sitting there, decaying politely. The ghosts of classes past left notes in penknife ink: C+L 4ever. Darren was here. Question Authority.

God, I wish I'd had the nerve to say half the shit they carved. Rebellion in carved wood.

Dom was with us too. He wondered if there were ghosts watching. Drew smirked, said they were probably just mad we found their hideout. Dom called it our hideout. And just like that, it was.

We laughed the kind of laugh you can't recreate once you grow up. That breathless, stupid, rule-breaking kind. The kind you carry with you long after the moment fades.

We spent an hour in there. Maybe more. Just soaking in what it felt like to be young and ungoverned. To be invincible. To not know that life gets heavier. That one day your memories will be the only thing standing between you and the abyss.

We never told anyone about locker 214. Not because we were being noble. It just wasn't theirs to know.

J.L. Jackson doesn't exist anymore. Flattened. Replaced. Just like everything else that once meant something.

But every time I drive by that street, I still see it. I still hear the creak of the floor, the whispered laughter, the faint echo of who we were.

And in some twisted, beautiful way, I feel okay. Like maybe life is just one long scavenger hunt for those moments.

And here's the kicker: Drew's still around. Same goofball. Same heart. We survived that place. We survived everything that came after.

These days, when the world gets loud (and it often does) I go back to that tunnel. I think about a rusted desk, a carved heart, a bad haircut, and a friendship that outlived everything else.

Claire's gone off on her own adventure now. Probably carving her initials into her own little corner of the world.

And me? I'm still here. Still smiling like an idiot over a memory that smells like dust and sounds like laughter.

It's amazing, the shit we keep in lockers.

# Milk Run Misfits and the Great Coccyx Caper

By the time I hit junior high, my adolescent brain had launched into full-blown delinquent freefall. I'm talking terminal velocity. Skip class? Check. Hurl rocks at freight trains? Repeatedly. Chug beer and stay up all night like a stunted Hemingway? Hell yes. My friends and I weren't just flirting with rebellion — we were dry humping it in public.

Why we thought chucking rocks at trains was so hilarious is beyond me now. At the time? It was lawless bliss. A middle finger to everything structured and safe. Somewhere in the mix, we also developed a taste for beer — usually stolen from my older sibling's stash. He never noticed. Or maybe he did and figured it was a small price to pay to not interact with me.

It was late in the school year. That time when the air starts to smell like summer and every lesson feels like a prison sentence. And right on cue, the school threw its annual tradition of hell at us... the Milk Run. Which, in case you're lucky enough to have avoided this masochistic ritual, was a day where they tossed students out into the sun to "run for a cause" and then stuff us full of milk.

Yeah. We weren't buying it either.

For weeks we whined about it like old men on a porch: "Why are we running? Who does this benefit? Why can't they just mail a check?" Eventually, someone, probably Dom, said what we were all thinking: We're not doing it. Full stop. Screw your run. Screw your cause. Screw sweating through our awkward puberty shirts in front of people we might one day want to ask out.

Now, I should probably date myself here. This was the golden age of The Jerky Boys — prank call pioneers — and the dawn of CKY, which later evolved into Jackass. Basically, the cultural blueprint for dumb teenage boys looking to weaponize boredom. We were devout followers.

We hatched a plan. The morning of the Milk Run, we'd all gather at my place — ground zero for most of our bad decisions, mostly because I lived closest to school and my house had a working phone. One by one, we'd call the school, impersonating our parents and calling each other in sick.

But we weren't idiots. We knew about caller ID. Enter star-six-seven-en. A prehistoric trick to mask your number like you were in the CIA.

The vibe was electric. Like Ocean's Eleven, if Ocean's Eleven was full of hormonal Canadian kids with zero cool and no backup plan.

The first attempt was a disaster. None of us could keep a straight face. Laughter exploded like an open soda can. Dom went first. He called in for Robbie, using an accent I can only describe as a horrifying blend of Eastern European meat vendor and a Minnesotan with head trauma. I had to bury my face into a pillow to keep from exploding.

He swatted at me like a dying fly, trying to hold it together. Somehow — somehow — it worked. Robbie was "excused."

Robbie then called in for Dom. He lasted three words before erupting into laughter. His laugh could raise the dead — the kind of infectious noise that would get you kicked out of funerals and elected as class clown in the same breath. But fate was on our side that day. Robbie regrouped and delivered a masterclass in adolescent bullshit.

Now it was down to Drew and me.

I stepped up. Lowered my voice. Took a deep breath. Called in for Drew.

"Yes, hello, this is Mr. (Redacted), Drew's father. The boy's got a fever. He's been puking all morning. Poor kid looks like death warmed over. I told him to stay home, but he's stubborn, that one."

They bought it. Another win.

And then... Drew picked up the phone to call in for me.

Now, I've known Drew since grade six. Which is to say, I know when he's about to do something stupid. He gave me that look — the one that said, Trust me... but also don't. I should've wrestled the phone from his hand right then and there. Instead, I let it play out like an idiot.

Ring... Ring...

"Hello, J.L. Jackson head office, how may I take your call?"

Drew, using the worst fake British accent this side of Monty Python: "Ah, yes. Hello. I'm Matthew's uncle. Poor boy won't be in today... hurt his coccyx at ballet."

My soul left my body.

"Bit of an aggressive arabesque gone wrong," he continued. "The lad landed square on his little dancer's tush during a grand jeté. You know how it is. Unitards offer piss-all protection these days."

By the time he hung up, I wasn't sure if I wanted to hug him or punch him. We were free, sure, mission accomplished. But now I was a ballet dancer with a bruised tailbone and a name in the dance community.

Fantastic.

Still, we were high on success. We hit the road toward the mall, ready to blow our newfound freedom on video games and greasy food.

But somewhere along the way, the euphoria started to rot. Every car that passed felt like an undercover teacher. Every glance from a stranger felt like an accusation. Then a police cruiser rolled by — probably just patrolling, but in our minds? Full SWAT team en route to bust the Milk Run escapees.

We cracked. Folded.

Dom, the voice of reason (which tells you how dire the situation was), suggested we just go to the damn run. And like the pathetic cowards we were, we turned around and joined the very event we orchestrated an entire con to avoid.

Worse still — we got called to the principal's office at the end of the day. Apparently, the secretary had noticed something odd in the morning call log. Maybe it was the fact every parent sounded like they were in witness protection. Maybe it was the ballet injury.

Whatever it was, the principal had questions.

Here's the thing though: we were present at the run. The attendance sheet said so. He had a list of fake calls, but no proof of our absence.

We walked. That slow-mo hero walk-out with a perfectly timed rock ballad playing in behind.

And that, folks, is how not to skip school, and why you should never let Drew make the damn call.

# Love Letters and Other Shenanigans

Everyone needs a friend who'll tolerate their nonsense. Not just tolerate — absorb it. Endure it. Nod through it like it's not completely unhinged. Sadly, not everyone gets that luxury. But I did. Actually, I still do.

His name's Drew. He's the kind of guy who's been around long enough to know all my worst stories — mostly because he was in them — and somehow still returns my calls. We met in grade six and never looked back. Not through cities, jobs, trauma, time, distance, or dysfunction. Some friendships fade. This one didn't. It just got stronger. Like a good single malt or a recurring back problem.

We did all the usual small-town shit: hockey, Halloween, beer theft from my older brother's fridge. We even got arrested together — light offense, don't worry. Some community service, a clown, and a poorly timed flirtation. That's a story for another day. The point is: Drew was there. Through it all. Every ill-conceived scheme I dreamt up, he followed with a grin and a bad idea of his own.

That's not friendship. That's brotherhood.

There's a strange kind of magic that happens when I'm around him. I don't feel like a man with bills and trauma and a browser history full of existential dread. I feel like a kid again. That awkward, skinny, bespectacled kid who still believed life might let him win.

Drew's been there for every meaningful chapter of my life. When I moved away and he started working, we kept in touch. When I started drowning in booze and all the demons that come knocking after midnight — he never walked. He didn't judge. Didn't sermonize. Just stayed tethered. Held the line. Hoped I'd find a way back to myself.

And I did. Eventually.

The night my mom died, Drew stayed on the phone with me. Not for five minutes. Not long enough to say "sorry" and hang up. Hours. From night into morning. No distractions. No checking the time. Just there. That kind of loyalty is hard to come by. Especially from a single dad juggling the chaos of his own life.

But that's Drew. Best of the best. Top-shelf human being. Probably doesn't even know it.

We all need a Drew. Most of us won't get one.

Stand by Me was one of my favorite movies growing up. Still is. There's something about the bond in that film — that tight-knit, ride-into-the-sunset kind of friendship — that felt familiar. Maybe it's the small-town thing. Maybe it's the part where none of the kids really fit anywhere else but with each other.

A few weeks ago, Drew and I hit the road to Castlegar. Impromptu trip. Five hours in a car talking about beautiful women, their criminally underappreciated... assets, and the general absurdity of life. Somewhere between the small talk and the big laughs, it hit me — I was making another memory with the one guy who's been in all of them.

You don't always know when a moment becomes a memory. But this time I did. I took a mental polaroid. Locked it away.

The trees outside were on their best behavior — emerald pines slowing down just enough to let us appreciate the drive. Rainy, overcast. My kind of weather. Melancholy with a soundtrack. Every second of that trip felt good. Not flashy, not grand — just good. Which, these days, is rarer than people admit.

Time doesn't make sense when you're with someone who knows all your chapters. In one moment, I'm that awkward kid again. In another, I'm a man sitting across from his equal. And somehow, both things feel true at the same time. The world softens. The noise dies down. And what's left is friendship in its purest form — no conditions, no qualifiers, just there.

Over the years, Drew's tolerated a lot of my bullshit. Sometimes he was neck-deep in it too, but he always had a way of dodging the consequences a hell of a lot better than I did.

We talk about love like it's this rigid, romantic thing — hearts and roses and grand declarations. But sometimes, love is a guy sitting next to you, laughing at your jokes, even when they're terrible. Sometimes, it's someone who doesn't flinch when you tell them who you really are.

When I was a kid, I didn't know what love looked like. My old man was a violent bastard who handed out pain like spare change. My mother — God love her — did what she could. But her love came with conditions: cigarettes, tea, rent money, errands. If I delivered, I got warmth. If not, I got called an idiot. "Stupid boy." I heard that more times than I care to count.

You know how many times Drew called me stupid?

Zero.

Even when I was. Especially when I was.

He showed me what unconditional love looked like — not in the scripted Hallmark kind of way, but in the real, ugly, beautiful, "you still good?" way. It changed me. Made me a better person. A softer man. Helped me trust a world that had only ever taught me to flinch.

So yeah — everyone needs a friend who tolerates their shenanigans.

Now you've met mine.

Thanks, buddy.

(And by the way... the Oilers still suck.)

Love,

A guy who knows the postseason only as a theoretical construct

— Go Sens Go.

# Fall Fair (With Apologies to Gravity and Good Taste)

A sunbeam ambushed me through a crack in the bleacher roof — a hot little bastard, searing my forehead like it had something to prove. I squinted, shuffled back, trying not to spill my tea or drop my breakfast sandwich, which, at that point, was the only thing tethering me to reality. I was alone, perched on those old wooden planks like some kind of broke philosopher, watching time unravel in the form of overgrown weeds and buzzing black flies.

The place had changed. Or maybe I had. Nature had done what it does best — taken over. Crawled and crept its way back through man's half-hearted attempts at permanence. But if you stared long enough, if you squinted past the decay, past the vines and rot and metaphor, you could see it — the place as it was. Like staring at a ghost in daylight.

I was time-traveling on a bench with egg in my beard.

The racetrack, once a hive of adrenaline and twisted steel, kicked off its blanket of weeds in my mind. I could hear the engines — Frankenstein'd together from lawnmowers and bad decisions — revving in my memory. That metallic scream of old cars fighting to die last. I could smell it too — dust, grease, fried onions, and the sweet stink of summer sweat.

The Salmon Arm Fair. My annual pilgrimage to freedom. A place where you could almost forget your life was a mess. Back then, it was a passport out of my own story — a temporary visa into a world where I wasn't the kid with a sick mom and an abusive ghost of a dad. I wasn't the boy in dollar store glasses or the one with bruises in places no one asked about.

At the fair, I was just a kid. Like everyone else. That's what made it sacred.

And autumn — God, autumn. That crisp flirtation in the evening air, hinting at the turning of things. It made the lights brighter. The rides faster. The cotton candy less disgusting. I always loved autumn. Still do.

And then came The Gravitron. That glorious, vomit-summoning death disc disguised as a spaceship. Imagine if a flying saucer dropped into a parking lot and said, "Hey, wanna question your bladder control?" That was the Gravitron.

We saw it — me, Drew, Dom, Robbie — our merry band of miscreants, standing wide-eyed, slack-jawed, and definitely not emotionally prepared. Dom, ever the poet, dropped a "Holy sh*t... let's do it!" and we were off. I followed like a lamb to slaughter, hiding my fear behind a shaky smile and the kind of bravado only prepubescent boys can manufacture.

Inside, I claimed my padded panel like a condemned man chooses his final meal. The darkness was my friend. It hid the fear-sweat. And boy, there was a lot of it. I was a human sprinkler.

Then came The Lock. A dull, cruel thud. No going back now, kiddo.

The announcer's voice oozed through speakers, warning us with cheerful sadism about what was coming. And then — music. Loud, abrasive, what-the-hell-is-this music. A whirring started. The ride rumbled to life. My stomach plotted its escape. But then — we rose. Up the walls. Sideways. Gravity bowed out and let physics have a go.

And I laughed. A real, guttural, forget-your-troubles kind of laugh. Because I wasn't dying — I was flying.

We tumbled out after, drunk on adrenaline and overpriced fair food, collapsing into laughter. We argued about which part was best. Which part made us gods. We did it again, of course. And again. Somewhere along the way, Dom figured out that spitting mid-spin was both disgusting and hilarious. Especially when your loogie lands on your best friend instead of your own face.

It was the best time of my life. And I didn't even realize it.

Flash-forward to now — back in the bleachers, my tea gone cold. I reached up, half-laughing, to check if I'd been spit on. I hadn't. Just memory messing with me again.

Nature had reclaimed the fairgrounds. The virus had canceled the joy. And there I was, stuck between nostalgia and melancholy like some sad narrator in a sepia-toned coming-of-age flick.

I wandered the grounds like a ghost in jeans. The place felt small now. But big in all the right ways. Because for once — just once — I got to feel normal. Not broken. Not damaged. Just a kid. A "real boy," if you'll forgive the cliché.

And sure, maybe you can't go home again. Maybe the fair won't come back, at least not like it was. But I have to believe it will. One day. The weeds will bow out. The laughter will return. The Gravitron will spin once more.

And maybe I'll ride it again.

With a face shield.

And a spare pair of pants.

Because gravity's a bitch. But memory? Memory is powerful mistress with whom I helplessly fall for when the sun hits just right.

# The Gospel According to Grass Clippings

Do you remember your first summer job?

I do.

Though full disclosure: between then and now, more years have piled up than I'm comfortable admitting. Years that snuck in while I wasn't looking, like hangovers after your thirties. But yeah, I remember. Fourteen years old, the summer of '97. The kind of summer that felt like it had been personally curated by Satan himself — blazing sun, zero responsibilities, and more boredom than a Sunday service with your grandma.

Back then, my biggest problems were avoiding chores and figuring out how to steal beer without becoming a headline. My best friend Drew and I had the system down: snag a couple cans from my fridge and make the hike up to the overlook trail behind my house. We'd sit on that hill like kings of nowhere, casting our dumb, naive eyes over the tiny town below. Thought it was boring. Thought it was small. Thought we were destined for more.

Turns out, it was beautiful. We just weren't smart enough yet to know it.

That summer was different. Drew got drafted into the family business by his parents — two suburban blue-collars with a laundry company. That left me alone most days, just a hormonal idiot meandering through town like some tragic Dickensian character in cargo shorts.

So, I joined the workforce. Enter: lawn care.

More specifically, enter *Old Man Thompson* — neighborhood cryptid turned reluctant employer. The guy lived in this rickety old house that looked like it had survived at least three apocalypses. He was a walking antique, thin as a whisper, with a face like dried leather and eyes that looked like they'd seen the invention of fire.

The man needed a kid to mow his lawn. I needed pocket change and maybe a little meaning. Thus began the most miserable, educational summer of my young life.

My first day, he handed me a gas can that probably dated back to the Cold War and pointed at a lawn mower that looked like it had a body count. "Knock yourself out, kid," he said, then walked off like a retired drill sergeant who'd just sentenced me to death by grass.

That lawn? A jungle. A knee-high, rock-infested wasteland that felt more like a metaphor than a yard. The mower bucked and screamed like it was possessed. Every push was a prayer. Every rock was a landmine. I was sunburned, sore, and convinced I was dying of heatstroke. I hated it.

And then came the lemonade.

Thompson, the grizzled bastard, would saunter out with a cold glass like it was a peace offering. We'd sit on his porch in silence, drinking in the shade while the world hummed around us — cicadas, distant lawnmowers, birds arguing in a tree somewhere. And for a few quiet minutes, life didn't feel so heavy.

He never said much. But when he did, he *really* said something.

Turns out, under all that crankiness and sun-bleached denim was a man who'd lived — like, *really* lived. He'd talk about his wife, long gone but forever present. He told stories about the war — the real kind, with blood and consequence. I sat there, nodding like a good kid, pretending not to be affected while secretly hanging on every word like they were gospel.

By the end of the summer, I had that lawn looking like a goddamn golf course. Thompson stopped smirking at me and started nodding. That was his version of applause. One tight, knotted handshake on the final day, and just like that, it was over. I had blisters, a wallet full of crumpled bills, and something new: the quiet understanding that hard work isn't about results — it's about *becoming* someone through the grind. Overcoming something that once seemed insurmountable.

He never said thank you. Didn't need to. The silence said it all.

Looking back now, that job was less about mowing lawns and more about shaping the edges of my character. That broken mower and I both had some growing up to do. And somehow, we both made it out intact. Mostly.

So here's to first jobs — to sweat, sunburns, and unlikely mentors. To the Old Man Thompsons of the world who show up just long enough to make a dent in your soul. To cold lemonade on hot porches and the kind of conversations you don't know are important until you're too old to have them again.

And maybe one day, if I'm lucky enough — unlucky enough — I'll be someone else's Thompson. Watching from a porch as some kid wrestles with life and a shitty lawn mower. Offering bad advice, good lemonade, and just enough quiet to let the lesson settle in.

Until then, I'll keep cutting my own grass — metaphorically, literally, emotionally. And I'll do it with just enough reverence for that first summer when I became a man.

Or at least a sweaty, stubborn approximation of one.

# How to Ruin a Summer and Remember It Forever

It was the last week of Jr. High and the summer before high school. I was fifteen — that awkward age where you're convinced you know everything while simultaneously scared shitless by the looming specter of algebra and adulthood. I was parked on top of a sun-bleached picnic table, Slurpee in hand, brain teetering somewhere between a sugar rush and a full-blown existential crisis. The sun had begun its daily descent behind the tree line, casting the sky in a shade of violet that would've made Van Gogh weep into his absinthe. And there I was, contemplating change.

Up to that point, my biggest ambition had been to one day marry Jordana Brewster or Katie Holmes — a noble pursuit, if I may say — but on that particular evening, reality decided to tap me on the shoulder. High school was coming. The beginning of the end. The last gasp of juvenile idiocy before society started handing out consequences with interest.

I mounted my trusty six-speed like some suburban Don Quixote and pedaled home, passing the fairgrounds along the way. I stopped, hand on the chain-link fence, staring into the empty lot. I could already see the fall fair rides in my mind's eye — the rickety Ferris wheel, the vomit-inducing tilt-a-whirl, the greasy-haired carnies leering through cigarette smoke. That place was sacred ground. A post-apocalyptic Eden for teens dodging parental curfews and seeking emotional refuge through sugar, adrenaline, and public groping.

I'd gotten into a fight there once — a shoving match, really. But when you're young, pride weighs more than truth. I claimed victory... She disagreed. (Kidding. I didn't fight a girl. I ran. Like a gentleman.)

Back home, I was struck by a lightning bolt of teenage brilliance — the kind that only hits when you're hopped up on high-fructose corn syrup and hormones. I grabbed the cordless phone — yes, we still had those — and dialed Drew. The Watson to my Holmes. The Goose to my Maverick. The poor bastard who always said yes.

"Drew," I said.

"Yes, sir," he replied, already wary.

"Bro, I've got a plan. A genius-level, post-pubescent masterpiece."

He sighed. Rightfully so. Most of my plans came with a side of grounded and a healthy dollop of property damage.

But this one — this one was special.

"What if we dedicate the rest of the summer," I said, "to adolescent delinquency? I mean, really lean into it. Make the most of the chaos before the state tries to domesticate us."

Drew paused. Then, as always, he folded like a lawn chair. "Sounds f***ing awesome."

The next day, we formed our council of idiots: Me, Drew, Dom, and Robbie. Steve was MIA, off with family or aliens or something. We planned the night like a military op — snacks, drinks, prank calls, and the pièce de résistance: calling Miss Cleo's psychic hotline and farting into the receiver. Because nothing says peak youth like passing gas into the metaphysical void.

I bet she never saw it coming.

Dom was the first to unleash hell. The moment was cinematic. The timing? Impeccable. Somewhere, a call center worker quietly reevaluated her life choices.

But the real chaos came when we decided to camp out at Drew's place, miles out of town. Hidden by trees and dusk, armed with a pile of baseball-sized rocks and the collective IQ of a wet sponge, we took to the bushes like hormonal G.I. Joes.

And then — the sound. That perfect symphony: the low growl of a semi barreling down the highway. Our cue.

Boom. Clap. Bang. The rocks struck the metal trailer like guerrilla warfare meets teenage boredom. We howled in delight. We were gods in the kingdom of stupid.

And then Dom — sweet, chaotic Dom — saw a Greyhound bus.

"No," we whispered.

"Yes," he decided.

He wound up like Nolan Ryan in heatstroke and launched a rock that shattered a passenger window and probably someone's faith in humanity. Sparks flew. Our freedom followed.

Cue the cops.

"Duck!" Drew yanked me into the bushes like some backwoods ninja.

Red and blue lights. Sirens. Shouting. Dirt in our mouths. Twigs in places twigs don't belong. Robbie and I fled into the woods, camouflaged ourselves in leaves and panic. It felt like *Apocalypse Now* but with more acne and less purpose.

Eventually, voices pierced the night. Drew's parents.

Game over.

We emerged from the shadows, dirt-covered and shame-drunk, and turned ourselves in like war criminals. Arrested. Cuffed. Taken downtown. My only request? "Can I stay in jail?"

I wouldn't see the guys again until after the weekend on the last day of junior high. We met outside school, all of us older somehow. Wiser, maybe. Not by much. Just enough to know that things were different now.

That start to summer was stupid. Beautifully, unapologetically stupid. But it was ours.

I did my community service at the fairgrounds — poetic justice, really. I even fell in love with a clown. A literal one. But that, dear reader, is a story for another day.

What matters is this: sometimes the dumbest things we do become the most unforgettable. And maybe, just maybe, that's the point.

Welcome to high school.

God help us all.

# Moonshots and Mummified Manhood

This morning, as I stood on my patio squinting at the sun like it owed me money, the heat rising from my coffee twisted into something more than steam — it became a time machine. One moment I was grumbling about the weather, and the next, I was fourteen again, standing in the blistering heart of a small town hugged by the Rockies, where trouble was currency and heatstroke was just part of the dress code.

Back then, summer wasn't a season. It was religion. Our gospel? Stupidity. Our rites? Pantsing ourselves by the railway tracks and baring our adolescent asses to an oncoming train like it was a rite of passage. Because when you're a bored teenage boy, and the town is too small to hide from your own imagination, you do dumb things. Beautifully, gloriously dumb things.

It was the summer before grade 10 — which felt monumental at the time, like we were ascending to some higher plane of locker hierarchy. My core crew rotated like planets around each other. If one wasn't free, another was. That summer, I hung out with Dom more than anyone. Lived just outside town, right on the tracks. It was the perfect setup for debauchery and bad ideas.

Sometimes, when his folks were out, we'd sneak into his dad's garage and borrow a couple clubs from his golf bag. Then we'd load up on rejected golf balls that looked like they'd survived a war, and head for the hill overlooking the bend in the tracks.

We didn't golf. Not really. We made commentary.

"He lines up for the shot. The crowd is electric. The weight of a nation on his shoulders. The backswing... the follow-through... BAM! That ball is a missile!"

The goal? Hit the train. Dead on. No points for distance, only impact. When ionomer resin kissed cold steel with that perfect hollow "CLANG," we'd howl like lunatics. It was a symphony of delinquency, and it was perfect.

One particular afternoon, Dom, Robbie, and I lounged under a maple tree, soaked in shade and bad decisions. I was nose-deep in an *X-Men* comic. The other two were in deep philosophical debate over optimal breast size.

"I'm telling you," Dom said, "anything more than a handful's a waste."

"Okay," Robbie countered. "So when you get your favorite meal, you only take one serving?"

"Hell no. I'm getting thirds."

"Exactly! Boobs are the greatest dish on Earth. You're saying one scoop's enough? Nonsense. The planet itself is shaped like a tit."

Dom lobbed a pebble at my shoe. "Matty, weigh in?"

I put the comic down, looked at both of them, raised my hands, and shaped the air with the universal gesture of teenage titty dreams.

"See?! Handful, told ya!"

"Bullshit!" Robbie fired back. "That wasn't a handful! Matty, back me up!"

I sighed like a man too wise for the debate he was stuck in. "Fellas... none of us have even seen a real boob. You wanna know the perfect size? The perfect size is whatever belongs to the girl dumb or kind enough to let losers like us anywhere near 'em."

We laughed because we knew I was right. And because laughter was our way of pretending we weren't virgins.

Suddenly, Robbie's head snapped to attention. "You hear that?"

We leaned in. Faint... but there — the telltale rumble of a train.

We were up like jackrabbits on Red Bull, sprinting through the trees toward the hill. No time to grab the clubs. No plan. Just instinct.

Which, apparently, led to us mooning the train.

There we were: pants around ankles, asses aimed skyward, giggling like idiots as a baffled conductor squinted through the windshield trying to figure out why the Canadian wilderness had grown butts. Robbie slapped his cheeks like a man possessed. Dom followed suit.

And then... he fell.

In his overzealous showmanship, Dom lost his footing and went tumbling down the hill like a flesh-toned tumbleweed of doom — all twigs, screams, and impending Darwin Award.

Robbie and I froze. Pants still down. Eyes wide. Hearts in our throats.

He was heading straight for the tracks. Where a train — a real one, not just a punchline — was thundering by.

Branches snapped. Twigs exploded. I thought we were about to become local legend: "Teen killed by train while pantsless. Ass was out. Dignity was not."

But nature had a sense of humor that day. Dom came to a halt just shy of tragedy, tangled in burdock and shame.

I ran down to check on him. "Dom? You alright?"

Just a moan. He was fine. Winded, scratched, pantsless. But fine.

And because we were teenage boys, this of course led to:

"Hey, Dom?"

"Yeah?"

"Nice cock. That come in men's?"

He looked down, realized he was still dangling out in the breeze, and laughed as he pulled his shorts up. That's friendship. That's love.

Later, back at my place, Robbie and I were playing *WWF Smack-Down* when Dom re-entered, fresh from the bathroom and looking a little... paler than usual.

"You good?" I asked.

He winced sitting down. "I think I hurt my dick."

Silence.

Then — howling.

"I cut it! I had a sliver!"

We laughed so hard I thought we might pass out. Between gasps he cried, "It's bleeding!"

Then he hit us with it: "Can you... ask your mom what I should do?"

This was no ordinary request. My mom was cool, sure, but there's a difference between 'can we drink in the basement' cool and 'help, my friend has a tree branch in his penis' cool.

"You want me to walk downstairs, look my mother in the eyes, and explain that you need first aid on your forest-fucked frankfurter because you rolled down a hill with your wang out?"

He nodded, dead serious.

I almost did it. I really did. But halfway down the stairs, I chickened out. Instead, I stood there in the hallway like a coward. Then I walked back upstairs and lied through my teeth.

"She said peroxide and gauze. Dab it like a bingo stamper. And if you don't, you'll get a man-gina."

"A... mangina?!"

"Yep. Like a reverse sex wizard. Just dip it and pray."

And God bless him, he did.

Robbie and I pressed our ears to the wall as Dom cracked open the peroxide. Then: silence. Followed by an unholy yelp and a thud.

Moments later, I found him in the bathroom. Pants down. Band-Aids and gauze wrapped haphazardly around his junk like King Tut's lesser-known cousin: The Pharaoh of Pubis.

"It worked," he whispered. "I'm not bleeding anymore! I gotta go thank your mom!"

And I, in one final act of betrayal, nodded.

"She's downstairs. She'd love that."

As he hobbled off to thank my unsuspecting mother for saving his dick — a conversation that surely left her puzzled for the rest of the day — I looked up at the sky, coffee now cold in my hand.

You know, I miss her. I miss those days.

And if you're wondering how that whole 'thank you' went down... well, that's a story for another time.

Until then — wear pants, stay off the tracks, and maybe keep a little peroxide handy.

You just never know.

# The Rumble

It was one of those days when the heat makes the pavement shimmer and your shirt stick to your back like bad decisions. The kind of July afternoon that feels like it was scripted by a guy who flunked out of film school but still swears he's got a masterpiece buried somewhere under a pile of rejection letters. Me? I was sixteen. Angry. Hormonal. Insecure. And despite my best efforts, I was about to get into a fight for the very first time.

Cue the western music — the kind with the whistle and the slow, tension-building guitar riff. The showdown was set. There we were, Drew on my right — my lifelong consigliere — and across from us, the living embodiment of a punchable face: Brad and his discount sidekick, Toby. The neighborhood bullies. Class-A degenerates with a PhD in public humiliation and a minor in being absolute pricks.

"You gonna run now, Matty?" Brad said, puffed-up and full of piss.

"Nah," I said, casual as a scotch neat. "I was just on my way to your mom's house. Service call. You know... routine maintenance."

Brad didn't like that. Go figure. The guy had all the emotional range of a traffic cone and half the charm.

"I'm gonna bash your fuckin' face in!" he growled, like that line had worked for him before.

"Some time this year, or...?" I quipped. My brain knew better. My mouth didn't care.

We were toe-to-toe at the mailbox near the end of my street. Classic suburbia battlefield — patches of scorched grass, a crooked post, and a lazy wasp orbiting like an omen. Drew and I had just been going for a walk. That's it. A goddamn walk. And then the storm rolled in wearing skate shoes and dad issues.

For years, these two asshats had made my life an open mic night for cruelty. They spit-balled my neck, whipped rocks at my back, turned dodgeball into artillery drills. But that day, something shifted. Maybe it was the heat. Maybe it was the presence of Drew — the human version of a lighthouse when you're lost in your own shitstorm. Whatever it was, I wasn't scared. Not this time.

"Enough talkin'," Toby squawked. "Why don't you just kiss my shoes and be done with it?"

"Well, Toby, I would... but it looks like your mom shops at Baby Gap. What are those, toddler size?" I said, grinning like the idiot I was.

Toby's face twisted — a Picasso of rage and confusion. He looked down at his feet, then back up, and lunged. That's when I let my arm fly — spaghetti noodle of a limb, flailing with all the fury of a wet paper towel in a wind tunnel. But damn it, I connected. Square on his jaw. I heard it — that sickening, percussion of fist meeting face.

Drew was already trading blows with Brad. My boy didn't hesitate. His knuckles said everything his soft-spoken heart never would. The whole thing lasted maybe ten seconds — two punches total, one each

— before we were all standing there again, panting, blinking in disbelief.

"You're lucky I don't beat your ass!" Toby hissed, bruised and embarrassed.

"Beat me?" I scoffed. "Bro, I just smacked you around worse than a pecker on prom night."

He didn't respond. He just turned and walked, dragging Brad and their wounded egos with him.

Drew and I stood there like statues left behind after a forgotten war. No victory dance. No backflips. Just the quiet buzz of adrenaline and the realization that we'd finally stood up for ourselves — or maybe, that I had finally stood up for myself.

We kept walking. Grabbed a Pepsi and a bag of All-Dressed chips — because in Canada, those are sacred. Made our way down to the wharf, sat on a busted old bench with rusted bolts and stories to tell. We didn't say much. Didn't need to.

Eventually, I turned to Drew and asked, "Did we... just get into a fight?"

"Yeah," he said. "I think so."

"And... did we win?"

"Yep."

"Holy fuck, Drew. We just got into a fight. Our first fight. And we fuckin' *won*! Dude, we got into a goddamn *rumble!*"

We held out our hands, side by side, red and trembling — matching badges of honor for boys pretending to be men. For the first time in my life, I felt... taller. Not because I'd punched someone. But because I hadn't run. And because Drew had been there, just like he always had.

That fight became legend. Each retelling got bloodier, louder, more cinematic. By the time it made its way through the friend group, you'd think we had been fighting off the entire Cobra Kai dojo.

Twenty years later, Drew came to visit me in Toronto. On a warm July day, we found ourselves at the corner of College and University, shoulder to shoulder again. Different city. Same brothers-in-arms but more grey hair. Another standoff was brewing... but that's a story for another day.

# A Dog Named Sadie

"Holy shit... RUN!"

That was the command, screamed at full volume, lungs ablaze, soul mid-panic. Autumn, twenty-two years ago. Crisp air, cracked leaves, and two teenage idiots on the run. For our lives, no less. And the worst part? I couldn't stop laughing.

Now, before we get to the part where death nearly claimed us — or at least nipped at our adolescent heels with big slobbery jaws — let me introduce you to my accomplice: Drew. My best friend. My day-one. The guy who saw me at my lowest, and worse — saw me in high school.

We came up together in the backwoods of small-town B.C., stitched at the soul by hockey pucks, late-night heart-to-hearts, and an alarming number of snacks and late night tea. I'm talking industrial quantities. His sleepovers were less "hangouts" and more "weekend-long sugar comas with movie commentary."

Fast-forward a couple decades. Life had happened — that bloated bastard of a thing — and we hadn't seen each other in seven years. No fights. No fallout. Just time doing what it does best: getting in the way.

He's in B.C., I'm in Toronto. But for one glorious weekend, geography got bent over the knee of fate and spanked into submission. Drew came to visit. Which, by our laws, meant one thing only: sleepover.

I was as giddy as a schoolboy on Mountain Dew and unresolved trauma. Drew was coming. The good Drew. The real Drew. Not the FaceTime version. Not the friend-shaped silhouette I kept in my memory bank. The flesh-and-blood original, complete with that flawless grin and the same posture he's had since puberty.

When he arrived, I opened the door and time folded in on itself. Sure, we looked older — a few grays, a few creaks, a few more reasons to hate gravity — but behind the crow's feet and dad jokes, I still saw him. My guy. The only person who could make me laugh during a panic attack or convince me that eating 400 M&Ms was "a spiritual journey."

We hit the streets, navigated the madness of the city, sweated through our clothes like nervous first dates. By nightfall, we were sprawled across makeshift bedding, limbs everywhere, talking shit and memory-lane surfing like two washed-up surfers reminiscing about one good wave.

"Remember theme nights?" I asked, voice already thick with nostalgia. That was our thing. Halloween meant horror movies and Charlie Brown. Christmas meant *A Christmas Story* and *National Lampoon*. And all year round meant tomfoolery with a side of bad decisions.

"Remember that prank call?" Drew asked. Oh, I remembered. We told some poor woman she'd won Canucks tickets. She called back and said she'd traced our number. Said she *knew* where I lived. I nearly pissed myself.

We laughed. Hard. The kind of laugh that makes your face hurt and your lungs beg for mercy.

Then it happened. The memory. *The* memory.

"Drew... do you remember Mr. Stinky?"

He froze. Took a beat. Then burst into laughter. "Holy shit. Yeah. Scary as hell. But funny."

Here's the thing about Mr. Stinky — and yes, that was his government-issued nickname as far as we were concerned. He was the local cryptid. Surly. Slouched. Lived in a house that looked condemned even when it wasn't. Trash on the porch. Newspapers stacked like he was prepping for an apocalypse. Kids feared him. We tormented him. Because kids are assholes with sneakers.

One particular Friday, we were headed to *The Little Store* — mecca of corner-store cuisine. Chips. Pop. Probably a candy bar with too many vowels. Along the way, we passed Mr. Stinky's. I spotted him on the deck. Drew smirked. I smirked. We dipped into the bushes like Navy SEALs armed with pebbles and poor judgment.

"Okay, he's out there," Drew whispered. "Let's huck and run."

Perfect plan. Foolproof. We were the *Ocean's Eleven* of dumbassery.

Drew went first — a scatter-bomb of pebbles sailing through the air. I readied my payload. I cocked my arm back. Then I saw it.

Not Mr. Stinky. Not the paper. Not even his unblinking stare.

No.

It was the dog.

A *new* dog.

"Oh, fuck. Stinky's got a dog."

"Holy shit, RUN! DREW, RUN!!"

We took off like two cracked-out gazelles. The beast behind us? To our minds: a hellhound sent by Satan himself. In reality? A friendly black lab named *Sadie*. But context is everything when you're a hormonal idiot convinced you're about to die.

I ran. I ran like I owed the universe money. Drew? Drew hit a gear previously reserved for Olympians and cartoons.

And me?

I laughed. Of course I laughed.

"Stop laughing and run!" Drew screamed.

"I'm trying! I'm gonna die laughing!"

We burst into the school through the side doors — open, thank God. We nearly gave a poor janitor a heart attack.

"No! You go! Not here!" she cried, gesturing like we were bringing in the plague. I tried to explain through wheezes and gasps that a demon-dog was chasing us. She looked out the window.

Sadie wagged her tail and barked, politely.

Yeah.

Eventually, we looped back through alleyways, dodged responsibility, and found ourselves at the store. Junk food in hand, hearts racing, egos bruised. We ended up at the wharf, watching boats drift and the sun set. And like always, we laughed.

"Oh, I should tell you..."

That monster? Mr. Stinky? His name was Harold. He became a family friend. Got help. Found peace. Befriended my mom. I even helped him move once. Sadie? She liked ear scratches and fries. No fangs. No bloodlust. Just love.

They're both gone now. And the only thing that truly stank? How we treated him.

But he forgave me. Let me tell him stories. And when I did, he smirked. The same way he did that day on the porch. Mischievous. Kind. Human.

That night, Drew and I laughed until we couldn't anymore. And when he fell asleep, I stayed awake just a little longer.

Thinking about dogs. About Harold. About being young, stupid, and gloriously alive.

And about how sometimes, the monsters from our childhood weren't monsters at all.

They were just people.

People who needed love.

And maybe... fewer pebbles.

"To be a paramedic is to drink inhumanity and never complain of its taste."

— Matthew Heneghan

# STORIES IN UNIFORM AND THE HUMAN BEHIND IT

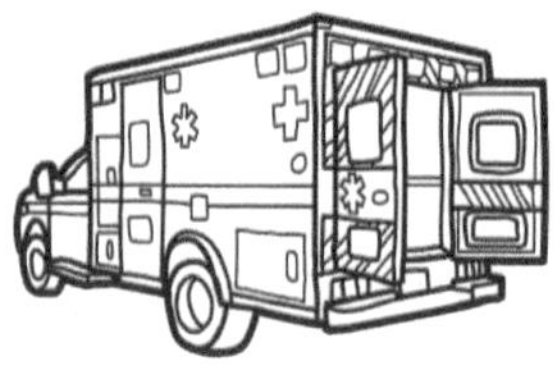

# CONTENT WARNING

The section that follows contains graphic accounts of medical emergencies, trauma, death, addiction, and mental health struggles drawn from real experiences in military and paramedic service. Some scenes involve vivid depictions of injury, loss of life, and the emotional impact of frontline work.

These stories are told truthfully and without embellishment, but they may be distressing for readers with personal experience or sensitivity to these subjects.

Please take care of yourself as you read. Pause when needed. Skip what you must. Your well-being comes first.

# Coffee, Codes, and the Reaper

There are nights, man... nights that wrap themselves around your ribs like a vice and never quite let go. Nights that don't fade into the rearview like they're supposed to. They don't dissolve with sleep or cheap whiskey. They haunt. They linger. They whisper.

Chris called it a "Big City Night."

Said it with that sun-kissed surfer voice of his, like he'd just come from riding waves instead of walking into chaos. Chris was joy wrapped in scrubs. The kind of guy who could find light in a blackout. Not because he was oblivious — because he was defiant. He didn't run toward misery because he liked it. He ran toward it because he wanted to beat it. One chest compression at a time.

We were partners. Not our first shift, but our first *code*. That's medic-speak for cardiac arrest — a living room showdown with the Reaper. Him, scythe in hand. Us, with drugs, wires, defibrillators, and a prayer. It's what we train for. Our Super Bowl. Our final boss fight. Most of the time? The Reaper wins. But we still show up. Every goddamn time.

That night was October's bastard child — all teeth and frost, and for reasons I still can't explain, our sleepy little town lit up like a crime blotter on fire. Death, overdoses, violence... all crammed into a single stretch of hours. Like the devil wrote the schedule and forgot to pace himself.

Chris and I were on call, and from the moment that first tone cracked through the radio static, we became the leads in a grim little indie film that no one paid to see.

"Big city night, Henny! We got ourselves a big city night!"
He said it with a grin, turning the keys in the rig like we were chasing something fun.

We weren't.

First call: an old woman crumpled on kitchen linoleum. Her soul had already clocked out, but we did the dance anyway. Because when family's watching, you perform. You lie with your hands. You buy time with empty CPR compressions. And then, when it's over, someone has to say the words out loud. Chris did it gently. There's no good way to tell someone their world just ended — but if there is, Chris was close.

We barely had time to toss the gear back in the truck before dispatch dropped the next hammer: young male, possible suicide by hanging.

Cue lights. Cue sirens. Cue chaos.

A woman came barreling out of the house like her grief had grown legs. Hammering on the window, yanking at my shirt, begging me to fix what had already shattered. I got stern — not because I wanted to, but because I had to. I don't like being grabbed. Not then. Not now.

We found him suspended in a closet. Chris and I got him down and started to work — lines, meds, shocks, compressions. He came back.

Then coded again at the hospital. Then came back *again*.

Alive. Broken. But alive.

We stopped for coffee at the only 24-hour joint in town — a Petro-Can that smelled like burnt beans and last chances. The coffee was terrible. Tasted like motor oil and resignation. But it was hot, and it was quiet. For a minute, anyway.

"Medic One, respond to unresponsive male, palliative."

Translation: someone dying the slow, legal way.

Chris looked tired. Not physically — spiritually. Suicide calls do that. They scratch the inside of your ribcage and settle in for the long haul. You don't feel it till later. Sometimes years later. Sometimes... never.

He took a sip of his coffee, grimaced. "Big city night, Henny," he muttered again.

We dropped a twenty on the counter and walked out. Didn't wait for change. You never do when you're chasing ghosts.

The next patient was already dead. On his own couch, the TV still playing, his wife — *widow* — insisting that he wanted to die at home. Away from fluorescent tubes and cold hospital trays. She sat with him while he went. That kind of love is rare. Beautiful. Brutal.

Chris and I waited for the coroner. The sun started to bleed into the horizon, washing the town in soft gold. But we were still stuck in the black-and-white reel of that night. We'd been to six or seven calls by then. I stopped counting. Time bends during those shifts. Stretches. Collapses. Morphs into memory and nightmare all at once.

That was 2008.

Chris went on to be a fire-medic in a bigger city. I traded sirens for sentences, my jump bag for a journal. We kept in touch. Shared beers. War stories. Laughed about the dumb stuff. Danced around the trauma.

On October 20, 2019, Chris took his own life.

I got the call while standing alone in a city that didn't care. Sirens howled in the background, and I remember thinking how poetic that was — the world still calling for help, even after one of its helpers had tapped out.

I didn't see it coming. I *should* have. I *should* have seen past the grin, the surfer charm, the endless quips. I *should* have noticed the cracks in the armor.

But I didn't.

And now, every October, I hear his voice in my head:

"Big city night, Henny."

Every time I hear a siren, I see his smile. Not the one everyone else saw — the one he wore just for me. Tired. Frayed. Brave. I see him on that night, when we were just two guys in a rig, trying to hold back the tide.

I miss him.

And every time I write about death, or love, or pain — every time I crack a joke in the face of despair — I think of Chris.

Rest easy, brother.

You fought the good fight.

And yeah...

It was one hell of a big city night.

# Between Flights and Farewells

"I get in shortly after eight your time... come pick me up and we'll hang out for a couple hours. It'd be good to see you, Henny."

That's what he said. Through the pinholes of my phone speaker, his voice poured in like sunlight through blackout curtains. I grunted some kind of agreement, promised I'd be there, then hung up and rolled onto my back.

Bad move.

Gravity had officially declared war on my insides. My brain throbbed against the walls of my skull like it was trying to file an escape plan. My mouth tasted like regret. My stomach was staging a coup. I took a deep breath, thinking maybe I could yogi my way out of this hangover.

Nope.

Cut to: me, sprinting to the bathroom like an Olympic hopeful, trying not to redecorate the floor with last night's whiskey sins.

After dry heaving myself into submission, I slumped against the cold bathroom wall, boxers twisted, dignity questionable. Glanced at my watch. Four hours until Chris landed. Four hours to go from hobo to highway-operational. Four hours to sober up enough to brave the 401, dodge airport parking extortion, and not puke on someone's luggage.

And yes, you heard me right — four o'clock. In the afternoon. That's when I was waking up. Not because I was lazy. Not because I was tired. Because I was broken. Life had curb-stomped me and I was trying to drink the bruises away. I'd quit my job, torched a seven-year relationship, driven across the country like a sad country song, and was now crashing on a couch that smelled like vintage despair.

Rock bottom? Not yet. But I could see the zip code.

Chris was one of the good ones. One of the real ones. We met post-military, both trying to survive life in small-town ambulance service. He had that firehouse optimism — all adrenaline, gallows humor, and the kind of loyalty that made you feel like you might just be okay.

First code I ever ran was with Chris. Kid made it. Which almost never happens. So yeah — we were bonded. Not just by trauma, but by the rare moments where you get to high-five Death and walk away.

Now, years later, he was on his way to Machu Picchu — one of those 'find yourself' trips people take before they realize the thing they're trying to outrun is strapped to their ribs. He had a layover in Toronto, and instead of sleeping or stretching or doing anything healthy, he wanted to see me. Of course he did.

And me? I was barely upright, nursing warm beer and shame.

But I pulled it together. Showered in my underwear. Got dressed like I was assembling IKEA furniture. Finished the dregs of a stale Molson, and made it to the airport just in time to dodge the lot Nazis and spot him through the crowd.

"Henny!"

"Chris."

He grinned like he always did — sun in human form. Then came the classic opener:

"Let's hit your place. I gotta take a creamy shit."

"Jesus, you saved that just for me, huh?"

"Like steamy soft serve, baby."

Nothing says "I love you" like a weaponized bowel movement.

Back at my place, he made good on his promise and nuked my toilet into a biohazard zone. It smelled like regret and gym socks had a baby. Then, mid-sulfuric haze, he rummaged through his bag.

"Shit... I forgot your fire shirt."

"No big deal, man."

"First beer's on me, Henny."

We hit a bar that looked like it hadn't passed a health inspection since Nirvana was still touring. Perfect. The band sucked, the lights flickered, and the beer was cold. We talked like no time had passed — war stories, jokes, future plans. He even tried to convince me to join him on his trip. Said he'd pay.

I wanted to say yes.

But broken men don't hike mountains. They order another round.

Then came the girl.

Hand on his shoulder, fingers tracing the letters on his "FIRE RESCUE" shirt like she was reading braille. "So... are you really a fireman? Or do you just like the costume?"

Chris puffed up, smiling like he was auditioning for a cologne commercial. But before he could answer, I stepped in.

"You know the Village People? He's in the tribute band."

Chris: "OH, FUCK YOU, HENNY."

We laughed like idiots.

Later, in the car, things got quiet. He had to go. We both knew it. Pulled up to Departures, did the man-hug thing.

"Hey, Henny..."

"Yeah?"

He started wriggling like a snake in a duffel bag, then peeled off his shirt. Handed it to me. "Take mine. Fire Rescue. Works on the ladies."

I stared. "You serious?"

"Dead."

It was the last time I ever saw him.

Years later, on a cold October day, Chris died by suicide.

He gave his life to rescuing others. But no one knew he needed rescuing himself. Not even me.

I think about that day often — that last layover. How he flew, and I stumbled back into the same bar as before. How I should've hugged him. Told him I loved him. Thanked him for all the things he never asked to be thanked for.

But I didn't.

I don't drink anymore. And I don't wear the uniform either. But sometimes, when the world is quiet and my mind isn't, I hear it — Chris clearing intersections, yelling through the cab, "Coast is clear, Henny! Hit it!"

I miss him. I always will.

I don't know what happens when we die. But I hope he's up there somewhere, fronting a celestial Village People cover band, pulling chicks and cracking jokes.

And if I listen close enough, I can still hear it:

"OH, FUCK YOU, HENNY!"

Yeah, love you too, brother.

Rest easy.

# Wishbones & Whiskey: A New York State of Mind

I once had a beer with Abraham Lincoln. Swear to God. Shared a pint with Charlie Chaplin too — Chuck, if you're close. Caught a glint of Houdini's old magic, the kind that makes you question reality and your place in it. I've rubbed elbows with suits and dignitaries, and I've clinked glasses with city rats who smell like cigarettes and broken dreams. How, you ask? Easy. I went to New York, baby. The city that never shuts the hell up. The year? 2013. The place? That's the story.

If you ever find yourself stumbling around the bottom end of Midtown Manhattan — dazed, hopeful, maybe a little hungover — do yourself a favor: head to 15 East 7th Street. There, tucked into the aging architecture like a secret handshake from the past, is a place so rich in history it practically exhales ghosts. You'll know it when you see it — green signage, black entryway, and outside, a couple of tipsy-looking kegs leaned against the wall like they're about to tell you a war story. McSorley's Old Ale House. Been serving trouble since 1854. They call it the oldest pub in New York. Bold claim. It's literally etched into the damn window.

Walk through the doors and it's like stepping into a sepia photograph. The place creaks under the weight of history. Sawdust carpets the floor like confetti from a drunken parade. The wood is warped, arthritic, like it's had its own hangovers. But don't call it a dive — it's not. It's a cathedral for the unshaven and the unquiet. A reliquary of every man who ever needed a drink more than a conversation.

The walls are stitched with old photos — loggers, sailors, forgotten men in forgotten hats. Honest Abe used to drink here. Houdini left a pair of handcuffs behind like a calling card. They're still hanging above the bar, untouched, like a promise or a dare.

They serve two things in this bar: ale. Light or dark. That's it. No hard seltzers, no pumpkin spice nonsense. You walk in, you get hit with the thick perfume of time and hops. You drink like a man with something to forget.

I was in a bad way that spring. Emotionally, mentally... spiritually, if you believe in that sort of thing. But my best friend Drew didn't mind. He never did. He flew in from the other side of the country for what we called our annual "bro trip." Sometimes life got in the way — his life, geography, my demons — but that year, 2013, we made it work. And there we were, two kids from nowhere, standing in the middle of New York City with our dreams and dysfunctions dangling out of our pockets.

Statue of Liberty? Sure, we saw it. Took the ferry out, tried to imagine what it was like for the broken and the brave who sailed here chasing hope. It was humbling. My own shit felt a little smaller for a moment.

But McSorley's — that's where the magic happened. Drew had done the research, found the pub, and dragged me there like a man on a mission. When we walked in, the place was shoulder to shoulder. Standing room only. We each grabbed two drinks because this wasn't a night for moderation. And that's when I saw them — the bones.

Wishbones.

Dozens of them, lined up on a beam above the bar like pale sentinels of forgotten hope. I asked the bartender what the deal was. He leaned in, wiped his hands on a towel stained with a hundred years of stories, and gave it to me straight.

World War I. McSorley fed every man headed off to fight. Turkey dinner and a pint. The soldiers left wishbones above the bar — a promise to return, a prayer for luck, for life. None of them ever came back for their bones. Not one.

And McSorley? He never took them down.

That's loyalty. That's reverence. That's a fucking gut punch.

I couldn't stop staring at those bones. All I could think about were the names — Starker, Boomer, Wilmot — the guys I served with, laughed with, bled with, and buried. Their wishbones were never collected either. But I knew what they would've wished for.

That night, the beer went down easy, like medicine or confession. Drew and I stood in a corner of that old pub, drinking like brothers, like survivors, like idiots with nothing to prove but everything to feel. He toasted the moment, and I toasted the ghosts. And for a few perfect seconds, the world stopped spinning. The pain went quiet.

So yeah, I've had a drink with Abraham. Shared silence with Houdini. Toasted to the unknown with a thousand men whose names history forgot. That's what McSorley's gave me — not just a drink, but a moment in time. A wishbone of my own.

New York never sleeps? Damn right it doesn't. Some places are too haunted to rest. To me, that's the true New York state of mind.

# August, You Bastard

August. A month that smells like encroaching pencils to some that fear back to school and death to others. For most, it's just sweaty skin and back-to-school flyers. For me? It's a slow-motion train wreck of memory. It's a month dipped in ghosts — the kind that don't rattle chains but instead whisper in your own damn voice.

See, August doesn't ask for your permission. It just shows up, drags you back through the worst parts of yourself, and leaves claw Radnors behind your eyes. There's no hiding from it. Beginning, middle, end — none of it negotiable. You just endure.

I'll give you an image: a bar. Not one of those polished, yuppie-friendly gastro-joints with reclaimed wood and ironic cocktails. No, this was a dive. A dump. A place with chairs older than most of its patrons and floors that gave up trying to be level sometime around forever ago. The kind of bar that looks like it's been abandoned by time, but serves modern booze. My kind of place. Because I didn't want to be seen, and I figured if the bar didn't give a damn about updating itself, it sure as hell didn't care about the sad sack drinking in its corner.

The day had been long. Hell, life had been long. I was slouched low, nursing something brown and familiar. All it took was a glance to the barkeep and the next drink would magically appear, like clockwork or magic — or alcoholism. An old tube TV hovered above the bar like some cursed relic. Dust covered, half-blinking. And then it happened. That damn screen flickered to life with something that made the room fall away: a funeral procession.

Soldiers. Marching. Flag-draped casket. The chyron screamed: *"FALLEN MEDIC, FIRST TO DIE IN COMBAT SINCE KOREA COMES HOME..."*

And just like that, the bar wasn't a bar anymore. It was a goddamn confessional.

One of the pallbearers caught my eye. Some gangly, barely-shaved grunt trying to hold it together. I squinted through the haze, heart already jackhammering, and I started laying into him. "You clumsy idiot," I thought. "You're screwing it all up. He deserved better." Every step the kid took was off-beat, like he'd never practiced the drill. I wanted to scream at him. I wanted to fight him.

And then it hit me like the business end of a Louisville Slugger: that idiot? That was me.

I was the gangly fuckup. The soldier who couldn't even carry a casket without falling out of step. The guy on TV. Frozen in amber. Failing on national broadcast while the rest of the world watched and went about their lives. No one in that bar recognized me, of course. I was invisible. Just how I liked it. Just how I hated it.

See, months before Cpl. Andrew James Eykelenboom — was blown out of this world, my own mother had stopped speaking to me. She called me selfish. A bastard. Hung up the phone on me and never picked it back up. So when Boomer came home in a box, and I was one of the eight tasked with carrying him... I had no one. No one to tell me I did okay. No one to tell me I looked strong. I was invisible to the world — and worse, to myself.

We made a pact, the eight of us. Not written down, not spoken in ceremony, but as real as anything: every time we touched that casket, we got shitfaced. Obliterated. Lost in the bottom of every bottle we could find. Because what else do you do when you're tasked with carrying a friend back from hell?

So that's the bar.

Now flash forward to the deck.

It's 2020, and I'm standing on my girlfriend's back deck in British Columbia. A gorgeous, postcard-perfect view of pines and spruce and mountaintops. And I'm staring into the woods, trying to breathe. But all I can hear is that goddamn rattle. The sound from inside Boomer's casket. I don't even know what made it — maybe dog tags, maybe something worse. But I heard it then, and I still hear it now. It's the worst sound I've ever known, and it plays in my head like a broken record the closer we get to August 11th.

Boomer was 23. Barely out of boyhood. But the stories they told about him — Jesus, that guy was a goddamn hero. He volunteered for that mission. He was done, off rotation, had the green light to sit it out. But they needed a medic and Boomer said, "I'll go." So he went. And a suicide bomber met him halfway.

His vehicle took the hit near Spin Boldak. Just like that, gone. He never came home, not really. Just his body, zipped up and silent. And us — the not-quite-ready, not-quite-sober pallbearers — we carried him. From Trenton to Comox. From war to rest.

We carried him drunk or hungover. Every single time.

But here's the thing: I made a new pact.

I carry Boomer differently now. I carry him in memory. In writing. In sobriety. No more drinks. No more dives. That guy — the one in the bar — he's dead too. That guy was no tribute. He was an anchor. I won't dishonor Boomer by drowning his memory in whiskey anymore.

So now, every August, I write. I tell his story. I remember. I thank him. I whisper his name to the wind and hope it finds its way wherever he is.

Boomer, you beautiful bastard — thank you.

Maybe someday, August won't feel like a punch to the soul. But until then, I'll keep showing up. I'll keep remembering. I'll keep carrying you.

Because you deserve that.

Rest easy, brother. Your war's over.

And if there's a Valhalla out there... I raise a glass (of water, of course) and say cheers to you.

# Dog Days and Dirty Boots

It was the kind of heat that makes you question your life choices — all of them. A sun so high and arrogant in the sky it felt like it was mocking us, daring us to drop dead just to give it purpose. August — nature's furnace with a side of existential dread. And there we were, five dumbasses with government-issued rucks, sweating like sinners in church, wandering through a patch of Eastern Quebec that looked like it had been forgotten by time and hygiene alike.

We weren't men. We were boys pretending, cosplaying adulthood with rifles and camouflage paint. Soldiers. Each of us had signed our names with the enthusiasm of drunks on karaoke night, convinced that joining the army was our rite of passage into something noble. Turns out, it was just our ticket to suffering under the blazing sun, tripping over roots, and getting assaulted by insects with a taste for misery and faces.

Private Blythe — or just "BlyBly" — was halfway to heatstroke, wheezing like a busted accordion. "Jesus Christ... I don't think I can go any further..." he muttered.

"Sure you can," Dieppe snapped, his sarcasm fried in French Canadian frustration. "Left, right, left. Tabarnak..." Then he crumpled to the ground like a man defeated by a cruel god.

We were supposed to be mastering topographical land navigation. Translation: Get lost with style. Our instructors, sadistic geniuses that they were, hand-picked the nastiest, most inhospitable points on the map just to watch us suffer. And suffer we did. We'd crossed a rope bridge that looked like it had last been used in the 1800s, tight-roped over a slime-coated log, machete'd our way through brush so thick I swear we could hear it whispering threats, and now we sat — exhausted and stinking — in a patch of forest that smelled like a fart trapped in a Tupperware left on a radiator trapped in an outhouse.

Lunch arrived in the form of vacuum-sealed disappointment. Blythe tore into his ration, took one look at it, and unraveled.

"Chicken A La King... again?! CHICKEN. A. LA. FUCKING. KING?!" He hurled the contents into the bush like a man casting out a demon. "How about Chicken A La FUCK YOU!" The bush swallowed it whole without protest.

We patched together a Frankenstein meal for him from our own rations, and for a moment, sat in silence, chewing the flavorless brick that passes for military food and reevaluating our decisions. BlyBly broke the silence: "My recruiter asked if I liked camping. Said this'd be like that. Fucking liar. This is The Running Man meets Predator."

I laughed. We all did. Couldn't help it. Blythe had that voice — a naturally funny cadence that turned even his rage into stand-up. Of course, that voice had almost gotten us both court-martialed during an inspection when my boot landed in his sleeping space.

The sergeant, a man forged from fire and caffeine, marched in, eyes like bayonets. He lost his mind over the state of my bunk, then locked onto Blythe like a predator spotting a limp gazelle.

"PRIVATE BLYTHE, WHY DO YOU HAVE HENEGHAN'S BOOT? FOOT FETISH?"

"SERGEANT, I BELIEVE IT FLEW IN HERE WHEN YOU LAUNCHED HIS BED, SERGEANT!"

"Oh, so it's my fault you want to tongue-punch his metatarsals, is it?!"

And just like that, I was in trouble again. Because laughter, much like chicken A La King, is hard to keep down in the army. BlyBly tried not to laugh. I tried not to laugh. We failed. Miserably. Push-ups were administered. The Queen was dishonored. Life moved on.

Later that day, we found ourselves neck-deep in swamp muck, trudging toward what was either another waypoint or the gates of hell. When we finally hit a patch of dry land, Blythe got stuck. Proper stuck.

"Fuck, I'm in quicksand or something!" he screamed, half-panicked, half-hysterical.

We should've helped. We meant to help. But someone yelled, "ARTAX!!!" — a perfectly timed Never Ending Story reference — and we were gone. Laughing like lunatics as Blythe flailed and cursed and threatened to murder us all in our sleep. I handed him a stick. Tried to be noble. But Heatley yelled, "Don't let the swamp get you!" and I collapsed in the dirt, tears streaming down my face, the sun now a distant second in terms of things burning me alive.

Eventually, we pulled him out. But the legend of "Nam... Farnham... doesn't matter, just listen" was born. Blythe favorite bar story. Mine too.

And then, just like that, it ended. Basic. The guys. The laughter. They disappeared, like most good things do — quietly and without ceremony. I never saw Blythe again. Or Heatley. Or Dieppe. But I think about them every time August rolls around and the sun beats down like it remembers who we were. I think of sweaty laughter and swallowed boots and the sound of "Atreyu" and "Artax!!" echoing through the trees.

I hope they're out there somewhere — on dry land, eating real food, telling war stories over cold beers, and still laughing.

God knows I am.

# New York, New York: How I Met Your Writers

New York. The Big Apple. Gotham. That unrelenting, unforgiving, wildly seductive metropolis that smells like ambition and piss — sometimes in equal measure. You don't visit New York. You survive it. You let it swallow you, chew you up, and if you're lucky, you leave with all your organs and maybe a story worth telling. This is mine.

It was 2013. My relationship was falling apart like a B-side Eddie Vedder ballad — sad, messy, predictable. I walked in on her wrapped around someone else like they were filming a live-action betrayal. She called it a misunderstanding. Said it was a hug. Lady, that's not how people hug — not unless they're trying to check each other for hernias with their hips.

So I did what any self-respecting emotionally stunted romantic does — I drank. Hard. Alone. At a bar I didn't even like the name of. Moxie's. Sounds like a dog's name. But the lights were low, the jazz was mellow, and the scotch tasted like forgetting. Somewhere between glass three and four, I texted my best friend Drew. Told him I needed out. Needed air. Needed the Statue of Liberty to whisper promises in my ear.

We booked flights to New York that night. A place we'd both always dreamed of visiting.

Cut to me stepping out of a cab in Midtown, and for the first time in months, maybe years, I smiled without pretending to. This city — God — it hits different. Like someone plugged your soul into a socket and turned the voltage up to "alive."

Drew met me out front of the hotel. The guy had that classic Drew grin — part trouble, part charm, all heart.

"Mr. Matt, we're in New York, buddy!"

Damn right we were.

We checked in, dropped our bags, and set out to do what we did best: wander aimlessly toward trouble. Trouble, as it happened, was located at 240 West 55th Street — McGee's Pub. A little Irish bar with enough television lore to make a grown man giddy. It was the inspiration for *MacLaren's*, the bar from *How I Met Your Mother*, a show that had become our post-midnight religion.

We stumbled in, eyes wide, hearts stupid. Red booths, low lights, cheap beer, and just enough sentimentality to make a guy like me feel things I usually drown. We quoted lines. Ordered rounds. Laughed louder than we should have. It felt good. Like maybe the past couldn't touch us here.

And then it happened.

Two guys sitting beside us talking shop about *HIMYM*. Drew, already three sheets to the wind and halfway through a hot dog he claimed was "spiritual," leans over.

"You guys fans of the show too?"

One of them raises his glass. "We don't just watch it... we write it."

We laughed. Of course we did. New York's full of guys who say they wrote something. Everyone's got a screenplay. Everyone's got a dream and a day job.

But then we Googled.

Carter Bays. Craig Thomas.

Holy. Shit.

There they were. The guys who wrote the damn thing. Sitting next to us. Drinking cheap beer with two schmucks from Canada who thought the highlight of the trip was going to be a slice from Ray's and a blurry picture of the Empire State Building.

We toasted. We drank. We laughed. We talked about writing, about heartbreak, about how some people look for love like it's oxygen and others run from it like it's a goddamn fire. They listened. Really listened. And I told them some of my truth — the dark, ugly, beautiful truth that hides behind polite smiles and work uniforms.

Then I noticed Drew was gone.

Cue panic. I searched the bar like a man looking for his last good decision. Found him in the basement bathroom, curled up like a drunk origami project, covered in a cocktail of regret and processed meat.

We staggered out of that place like soldiers returning from war. Drew painted the sidewalk with a Jackson Pollock of everything he'd consumed that day. A cab saw us and did what any sane New York cabbie would — peeled off like we were radioactive.

So we walked. Arm in arm. Through the streets of the city that never sleeps, lit by neon and shame. The lights spilled into the sparce puddles along the gutters like melting Skittles.

And you know what? It was perfect.

That should've been the end. But life — when it's good — knows how to throw in a third act.

Carter and Craig? They weren't done with us. Invited us to one of their favorite restaurants. BLT Steakhouse. We walked in like kids sneaking into a grown-up party, expecting the bill to bankrupt us. But when we asked for the check, the waiter smiled.

"It's already been taken care of. Mr. Bays and Mr. Thomas send their regards."

Drew and I just sat there, two idiots from nowhere, basking in the warmth of New York kindness and high-end beef.

We stayed in touch with Carter and Craig. They even invited us to the *HIMYM* finale at McGee's. We sat at the writer's table. Us — *me*. At the writer's table.

But that's a story for another night, another drink.

So what's the moral here? Maybe it's this:

Heartbreak will gut you. It'll rip you apart in a way no surgeon can stitch. But sometimes — if you're lucky — the universe gives you a break. A trip. A bar. A friend. A night you never saw coming. Sometimes, it gives you Carter and Craig.

And sometimes... it gives you New York.

# Half a Head and a Full Bottle

By 2012, I was rusted. Not metaphorically — I mean clinically, cosmically corroded. If sanity were a set of brake pads, mine had long since been ground down to metal. I was showing up late to work, calling in sick so I could get drunk, then drinking at home to sleep off the memories that haunted the dark. Spoiler alert: the memories always won.

I was surviving on a cocktail of nightmares and vodka. The ghosts didn't just whisper — they screamed. The worst part wasn't even the yelling. It was the smell. Memories have smells, you know? They crawl into your sinuses and squat there like they pay rent.

One early morning — the kind where night still hangs around like a party guest who doesn't get the hint — my partner and I tapped out early. We'd earned it. Our last call had been some twisted Picasso of carnage: a white pickup truck doing warp speed through the city's south end before deciding gravity was optional. It rolled. Violently.

Elegantly. Tragically. The truck looked like it had been on the losing end of a bar fight with a freight train.

Parts of it were scattered like a fucked-up scavenger hunt — hubcap here, muffler there, bumper halfway to Saskatoon. And the light pole? Bent like a drunk yoga instructor.

"Jesus," Witter muttered. "To bend one of those? Guy must've been doing Mach 2."

I pulled out my Maglite and shone it down the hill. Grass slick with dew. Blood-slicked airbag in a wheel-less wreck. I shouted down to the corpse on autopilot: "Paramedics. Don't move." As if that would matter.

Got closer. Peeled back the bag. Found what was left of the driver. Half a head. Bone, brain, and what looked like the inside of a ravioli exploded across synthetic fibers. A still life of trauma.

"Patient found. No transport — deceased," Witter quipped like it was the punchline to a sick joke.

We weren't laughing.

Then came the cop — too late to stop her from stepping into the visual blender. "Oh, *fucking gross!*" she gagged.

"Yeah, sorry. I was gonna warn you," I said, but it felt hollow.

She got our badge numbers, made small talk about having a good night — like this was some customer service interaction and not a bloodstained rendezvous with fate. We half-laughed again. Coping. Pretending. That's what we do.

Climbing back up to the road, my flashlight caught something. Grey. Pink. Pitted. Not asphalt — not quite. A chunk of brain. Just sitting there like a leftover from a dinner no one wanted.

Then another cop walked right into it.

"Fuck's sake... I just polished these boots," he groaned, like the real tragedy here was the brain on his leather.

"Isn't that always the way," I offered, because what the hell else do you say?

We drove back to base in silence, marinated in what we saw. Witter said we should call it — pack it in. I agreed. No debrief. No shrinks. Just get us the fuck out of this shift.

But I didn't go home. Home meant pretending. Instead, I went to see Marshall. He was a military guy, Irish stock. The kind of man who could turn a Tuesday night into a whiskey-fueled therapy session.

He was throwing a party. I could hear the music as I pulled up. But as I got out of my car, something felt off. Something in my boot. I thought it was a rock. Spoiler alert: not a rock.

It was a piece of skull. Human fucking skull. With brain matter clinging to the tread like some grotesque souvenir. My boot looked like it had stomped on a deli counter.

"Fuck me," I muttered.

Marshall must've seen me loitering because his door flung open. "My son! Git in here! There's a beer waitin'!"

I shook my head. "I can't."

"Why the fuck not?"

"Because I've got fuckin' brain on my boot."

He paused, the way only an Irishman can, processing it like a Zen koan.

"Well, fuck it then... we'll drink outside."

And we did. Two men, one boot full of trauma, laughing at the absurdity of it all. We drank until laughter made more sense than tears. That's the magic of dark humor — it's duct tape for the soul.

Eventually, I went home. Not to bed — not to *her* bed. I slept in the guest room. Alone. On purpose. I sat at the edge of the mattress with a phone in my hand, booze on my breath, ghosts in my head.

I wanted to call Colin. He'd know what to say. He always did. But dead men don't answer phones.

It had been four years. And still, all I wanted in that moment was to make one call I couldn't. The one that would make it all okay again.

It's not the calls we take that haunt us.

It's the ones we can't make.

# The Month That Stole My Brother

July. The month that shows up like an old flame with a scorched-earth heart and a grudge it never quite got over. It doesn't knock. Doesn't call ahead. Just kicks the door in and reminds me of everything I've tried not to remember. And it's not the whole damn month, really... it's just the 6th. A number on a calendar that hits like a bottle to the back of the head. July 6th. The day everything stopped making sense.

The day Colin died.

When I was 18, I signed up for the army like a kid picking a college from a brochure. Adventure, glory, the myth of becoming a man — I wanted all of it. What I got was dirt, blood, and brothers. Real brothers. The kind that don't care about your family tree, just whether you've got their six when the world goes sideways.

Colin was that kind of brother.

I met him after I got posted to 1 Field Ambulance — Canada's answer to the question: "How many medics can you throw at a broken world before someone snaps?" I'd already been there a while when he showed up. And just like that, the energy shifted. The kid had a crooked smile that could disarm a landmine. He was sunshine in a uniform, and somehow, he didn't make you want to punch him for it. You just liked him. Everyone did.

He wasn't loud. He didn't peacock. He just had this gravitational pull, like maybe the universe had made one decent man and then forgot to make more. I was a mess — tangled up in some rom-com-turned-horror-show of a relationship with a woman who loved to hate me, and made a sport out of doing so. And I was addicted to her like any bad habit. And one day, after a sweaty morning of punishment disguised as PT, we were sitting outside the barracks, and he said something simple that hit like a freight train.

"You don't deserve that, man. You're a good guy. A good-looking fella, too."

Now, I've been called a lot of things — some of them flattering, most of them not — but no peer, no man had ever said something like that to me before. Not with sincerity. Not without a punchline loaded behind it. But Colin meant it. That was his whole deal — he meant everything he said. And I, being the emotionally constipated, self-loathing twenty-something I was, laughed it off. And stayed right where I was — with the woman, the chaos, the slow bleed of my own damn soul.

I got out in 2008. Told myself it was to save the relationship. Spoiler alert: it didn't. Colin stayed. He deployed that summer. Afghanistan.

A few days after my discharge, the phone rang. Some official-sounding voice from the base telling me to report for parade. I reminded them I was done — civvie street, baby. He told me to disregard the order and said nothing more to me. Didn't have to say it. I already knew.

You don't get summoned like that unless someone's dead.

I found out from another buddy, one who wasn't too big on protocol and couldn't keep the tremble out of his voice.

"It's Colin."

And that was it. Just a name. A guillotine in syllables.

He was gone. Blown out of the world in a country where some argue that we should never have been in to begin with. A kid with too much light in his chest for a job that feeds on darkness. And just like that, everything tilted. Everything broke.

There's a special kind of grief that comes with unfinished conversations. I never got to tell him I listened. That I left her. That I found something real, something that didn't come with conditions or collateral damage. That I finally understood what he meant, all those years ago on that bench.

Now, every year on July 6th, I tell my wife and mini-humans about him. I make them listen, even when it hurts. I want them to know who he was... how his laugh sounded like the start of a good night, how he gave advice without turning it into a sermon. How kindness, real kindness, wore combat boots and had blood under its nails.

Private Colin Wilmot. Killed in action, Afghanistan, July 6th, 2008.

Always remembered. Always missed.

Every July, I remember a little too much, I cry a little too hard, and hate that I still have to write about him in the past tense.

But I try to corral that melancholic reality in a neat fold of a shinier perspective. I tell myself how lucky I was to know such a man as Colin. Truly among this world's very best. And not everyone is blessed with the chance of meeting someone like that. But I was.

That's how I get by. By reminding myself how lucky I was back then, and how fortunate I am even now — to have known a giant among men. To be able to take the ink of a pen and turn the cursive of my blood and tears into story and share it with the world.

My hope is that by sharing these stories; by telling the world of Colin, that for just a few more flickering moments of time, he gets to live once again.

Unlike a scorned ex-lover, every time Colin comes around for a visit, knocking on the halls of my wounded mind, I smile through a tear. Because I had the privilege of calling that man my brother.

And if you've read this — he's yours now, too.

# The Screams Never Stop

04:30 in the morning. That's when it starts. Again.

She's screaming. Not Sheena — not the love of my life — but *her*. The woman from a lifetime ago who died screaming and took a piece of me with her when she did.

It's not the kind of scream you can forget. It doesn't fade with time. It doesn't soften with distance. It stays sharp. Like a shard of glass you keep stepping on because you're too damn stubborn to admit you're still bleeding.

PTSD? Yeah, I've got that charming little souvenir. It doesn't knock. Doesn't flirt. It just barges in wearing boots, pissed off and ready to redecorate the inside of my skull. It doesn't give a damn how good your evening was or if the person next to you is the best thing that ever happened to you. It just shows up like an angry god in a low-budget Greek tragedy.

So there I sit — soaked in sweat, perched on the edge of the bed like a man exiled from his own mind. The world is asleep. Sheena's beside me, her breaths soft and steady. Gertie, our brindle bug, curled into the safety of domestic peace. They sleep, and I sit. A castaway in a choppy sea of memory.

I try. I really do. Gratitude, they say. Think of what you have. Count your blessings like rosary beads. I whisper silent thanks that I'm here and not *there*. The place with blood and sirens and the taste of failure in the back of my throat.

But try as I might, the screams cut through.

We weren't even dispatched. That's the cruelest part. We weren't called to save her. We found her by accident. Fate's twisted sense of humor. I spotted her — just a flicker of something not right out the corner of my eye — and told Radnor to turn the wheel. Rear lot. Industrial husk of a building. Steel steps, sharp angles, and a woman who'd been beaten until life barely recognized her.

She was street-tough, sure. Probably used to rough nights. But nobody's meant to be thrown away like that.

Nobody.

She fought us. Not like a villain — more like a scared animal. She spat, clawed, kicked. I didn't take it personal. I just held her hand. Told her she was safe. Lied through my teeth.

She coded the second we hit the ER. Lights, movement, latex hands doing a ballet of desperation. I watched them try. Watched her leave. Watched the doctor call TOD (time of death) like he was ordering breakfast. I stayed in that room long after the show was over.

I don't know why. Maybe I thought someone would come looking for her. They didn't. No sobbing mom. No strung-out boyfriend. Just me and a dead woman who hated me for trying to help.

I stood there with nothing to offer but silence. Words are useless in moments like that. Platitudes are for people who haven't seen the world eat its young.

Radnor came back in eventually, holding a cup of coffee that was actually steaming. A minor miracle. He handed it to me without a word. That's what partners do — they hand you the warmth when the cold won't let go.

I took a sip. It was perfect. Bitter and strong. We didn't get to enjoy it. Dispatch squawked and sent us on another call. The coffees sat in their holders, destined to become stale reminders of a moment almost had.

That's how it goes.

The screams don't stop. But neither do we.

PTSD has taken a lot from me — sleep, peace, any hope of enjoying fireworks or car backfires — but it doesn't get to have everything. It doesn't get to win.

Because even when the nightmares are loud, I wake up next to love. Even when my hands shake, they still reach for the light.

Even when the screams don't stop...

Neither do I. One step at a time, I walk myself further from that blood-soaked life. And if one step is too far, then I still manage forward crawl, one written line at a time.

# The Night DJ

There's something about the night — that sly bastard — that convinces you you're the last living soul in the entire goddamn universe. Everyone else? Sleeping peacefully, dreaming of grocery lists or missed connections. But not you. No, your mind decides now's the time to run back the highlights of every personal apocalypse you've ever lived through.

PTSD, they call it.

Post-Traumatic Stress Disorder.

Sounds like something you could organize with a filing cabinet and a prescription pad. Flashbacks go in this drawer, nightmares in that one, and—ah yes—let's alphabetize the panic attacks for easy access.

But it's not that clean.

It's jazz — chaotic, unpredictable, sometimes maniacal genius, mostly noise. It's static inside your skull, a broken record of screams and sirens spinning at 3 A.M. like some deranged DJ who only plays the songs that ruin you.

And here's the kicker:

I used to *like* the night.

I *chose* it.

Graveyard shifts. Midnight runs. I was like a trench coat-clad Batman with a stethoscope and a pocket full of Ativan. The streets made sense back then — or at least they didn't pretend to be something they weren't. Shadows were honest. Monsters weren't hiding, they were waving.

But now? Now the night feels like a fucking setup. A trapdoor made of silence and memory. The darker it gets, the more I feel those old ghosts stirring — in the corners of the ceiling, in the spaces between the floorboards. It's no longer peace and quiet. It's *just* the quiet. And that's when it hits hardest.

Funny thing about trauma — it doesn't care how old you are, how many medals you've got, or how many bodies you've zipped up. Forty-one years on this planet, served my country, served my city, and I'm still afraid of the dark. Not metaphorically. Literally. I'm talking lights-on, door-ajar, 'just-in-case' scared. I'm talking about a man who's seen too much and still gets spooked like the kid version of himself hiding under the blanket, hoping the monsters lose interest.

And tonight? Sheena and Gertie are gone. I'm flying solo. Just me and the ghosts — a classic Heneghan Friday. The temptation is to spiral. To pour a drink I don't drink anymore. To hit rewind and let the DJ do his worst.

But maybe — just maybe — I don't have to dance to every fucked-up song that plays. Maybe I can change the station. Maybe I can write my own soundtrack tonight. Something quiet. Something new.

Because here's the truth: I've made it through worse nights. Nights colder, darker, lonelier. Nights where I didn't think I'd see morning — didn't *want* to see morning. And I did. I *always* did.

So yeah. This night? This haunted, empty, creaking-floorboard night?

It's just another one.

And I'm still here.

And tomorrow — tomorrow there'll be light. The sun'll punch through the blinds like a golden middle finger to the dark. And I'll be there to flip one back.

So goodnight, ghosts. Goodnight, demons. Goodnight, insomnia and cold tea and all the things I can't forget.

And to you, dear reader — may your dreams be soft, your sheets be warm, and your monsters leave you the hell alone.

I'll see you in the morning.

# Ghosts Don't Knock

Being a paramedic isn't just about lifting stretchers and jabbing needles into arms. It's about what comes home with you — the stuff you don't pack, but carry anyway. Invisible passengers. Some of them ride shotgun for a while. Others find a way to let themselves in years later like ghosts with perfect timing and no manners.

This morning — 04:13 to be tragically precise — I woke up to the sound of an old woman crying in my bedroom.

No joke. No dream logic. Just *sobbing*. Full-bodied grief echoing off my walls like some kind of spectral voicemail I forgot to delete.

I sat up, sweaty and startled, doing that frantic scan of the shadows, looking for the source. I wasn't alone. At least not entirely. Because there she was — flickering in memory, more vivid than reality most days — the woman from *that* call.

It was spring. Barely. One of those Canadian mornings that promises flowers but still kicks you in the teeth with frost. The sky was a color only sad poets and unpaid artists bother to describe. Pale. Sickly. Ashtray grey.

She had called 9-1-1 because her husband wouldn't wake up. But he was still breathing when she called — that much I remember. The dispatcher tried walking her through CPR. And this tiny, silver-haired matriarch — powered by love or desperation or both — tried to drag her breathless husband from bed. I imagine it looked like trying to pull a tree trunk through molasses.

When Radnor and I got there, the man's body was half off the bed. His legs still tangled in the sheets like they didn't want to let go. His chest was pale, waxy, not fooling anyone.

We moved fast. We always did. Carried him to the living room and got to work — compressions, tubes, lines, stickers, drugs. All of it. The usual circus. And just out of view, this woman cried in a way that split the air. You can always hear it. Doesn't matter how many rooms away they are. Grief has a frequency that slips past walls.

Every time we pressed on his chest, she'd let out a sound like something ancient was breaking. And when the cavalry showed up — fire, backup units, the whole damn alphabet soup of lights and uniforms — I knew we were just dressing a wound we couldn't close.

When it was over, I walked to her. She didn't need words — not really. But I gave her the only ones I had:

"He's gone."

And she shattered like something priceless in my hands.

Let me tell you something — the screams of someone newly broken? They don't just bounce off walls. They lodge themselves in your chest. They take up residence in the air around you. And sometimes, if you're really lucky, they wait a decade and show up in your bedroom like a greatest hits track you didn't ask Alexa to play.

The worst part? It wasn't a memory. Not really. It was *now*. The sound of her heartbreak was *now*. The feel of his stiff chest beneath my gloved hand was *now*. The bristle of his wiry chest hair pressing through latex — still *now*.

These are the souvenirs nobody talks about. Not the medals. Not the handshakes. Not the plaques that sit in drawers.

Just echoes and ghosts and a morning where tea feels like the only thing strong enough to pull you out of the undertow.

So yeah — time for tea.

In a well-lit room. With doors open. Windows wide.

Because some mornings, the dark is too damn familiar.

And some ghosts don't knock.

"I don't believe in getting over things. The loss of a loved one, trauma, abandonment — you never get over these things. You get through them."

— Matthew Heneghan

# The Other Things

Sometimes, it's not the corpse that gets you. Not the bloated, blue-tinged body slumped in a kitchen chair, marinating in the stench of his own quiet demise. It's not the maggots or the smell or the way time turns a man into meat. No, sometimes... it's the *other things.*

It was one of those sticky summer evenings that felt like the city was trying to sweat out its sins. The sky had gone magenta, bleeding color like a bad memory. I was with Radnor—my partner in crime and caffeine abuse—parked roadside in our mobile sarcophagus, pretending we weren't dying inside from the heat. I was wearing ballistic plating under a poly-cotton blend uniform tailored by Satan himself. I hated summer night shifts. Always have. Always will.

"You catch the Jays game?" Radnor asked between expectorations of chewing tobacco into a plastic bottle he carried around like a disgusting adult sippy cup.

"Nope," I grunted. "Tried to sleep. Neighbors had a lawnmower symphony all goddamn afternoon. Sounded like a NASCAR pit crew on meth."

He nodded. Not an apology. Not even sympathy. Just... acknowledgment. It's a medic thing. The silent camaraderie of shared irritation. Daywalkers — people with routines and daylight and regular lives — they don't get it. But Radnor did. We both rode the vampire bus, working nights, dodging sunrises and streetlights.

Then dispatch broke in, her voice metallic and bored:

*"Alpha One-Nine, welfare check at 5601 Lincoln Way. Caller hasn't heard from her dad in a week. Lives alone. Health issues. Wife passed last year."*

Radnor started the rig. Diesel coughed. Sirens howled. Off we went, our red and white strobes painting misery across convenience stores and cracked sidewalks. I caught a glimpse of myself in a shop window as we flew by — ghostly and tired, a reflection dressed up like a hero but hollow behind the eyes. It's a weird thing, recognizing yourself and not recognizing yourself at the same time.

We reached the address. Quiet neighborhood. Sirens off. The engine idled like it knew something we didn't. Radnor and I scanned the houses, our breath catching a little as the numbers ticked closer.

"There it is," he said. "Second from the end."

"Awesome. Let's go see who forgot to keep living today."

We grabbed the gear. Standard issue trauma bags, O2, cardiac monitor. The stuff of miracles, usually used too late. But even before my boot hit the sidewalk, the smell hit me first — that dense, oily funk of expired humanity.

"Oh, *fuck*," I choked, trying to bury my face behind a gloved hand.

"Bloater?" Radnor asked casually, like he was betting on the ponies.

"At least." I nodded, already bracing myself for what was behind door number one.

I knocked anyway. Habit. Courtesy for ghosts. "Paramedics!"

Radnor smirked. "Little late for that, partner."

The door creaked open like it knew it was about to confess something.

Inside was... stillness. Not peace. Just sickened stillness. A haunted quiet. The kind of quiet that settles after all the crying is done. My fingers found a light switch. The hallway lit up, revealing a house frozen in time — threadbare furniture, faded photos, a fireplace with nothing left to burn.

It smelled like loneliness. It looked like it too.

The kitchen was worse. Laminate floor. One man. Dead. Bloated. Seated at the table like he was still waiting for breakfast. The plate in front of him had gone bad — like everything else.

And then I heard it.

A sound I'll never unhear.

A soft whimper.

Not human. Not quite. But absolutely soaked in sorrow.

Beyond the kitchen, in a dim hallway near a sliding door, was a dog. Golden retriever, I think. Or something that used to be. Skin hanging off bone, ribs like piano keys. Too weak to move. Too sad to care. Just... there. Lying beside an empty bowl, dying slower than the man had. Dying with a soundtrack. Whimpers that sliced through the silence, right through my Kevlar soul.

Radnor touched my shoulder. I jumped.

"Cops are coming," he said. "You good?"

No. Not even a little. But I said: "Yeah."

We radioed it in. Sat in that kitchen, surrounded by death and rot and the sound of a dying dog who never left his post. The kind of loyalty that breaks you. We didn't talk. We just... *were*. Sitting there, waiting, breathing in the worst parts of life and doing our best not to look at each other.

I don't know what happened to that dog. Maybe animal control came. Maybe they didn't. I like to think someone showed up and saved him. But hope is a currency I don't carry much of these days.

The corpse doesn't haunt me. Not really. I've seen too many to mourn the shape of death.

But the dog?

Yeah.

The dog stays.

Because sometimes... it's the *other* things that are the worst. Not the blood and guts from the movies. That shit's fine by me. It's the intangibles. The ghosts in the corners of rooms, the smell of someone's bad cooking that conjures memory you simply cannot share, and stale whimpers of man's best friend. That's the shit that sticks.

# SHANIA!

"No, no, pin it! Just fucking pin it!"

The Italian deathtrap we were in — an M40 military ambulance that looked like it had been through every war since Caesar — let out one last asthmatic cough and died on the muddy hill.

"Shit! Well, we're done. We ain't movin'," came Liam's grumble — a man carved out of cigarette smoke, bad decisions, and saltwater. He was in his sixties, spoke like a dockside philosopher, and wore his contempt for incompetence like it was issued with his uniform. I was behind the wheel, feeling that particular kind of guilt that only the powerless feel — not my fault we were stuck, but I still felt like I'd personally betrayed the Queen, the truck, and probably Liam's mother.

Liam threw his door open like it had insulted him, the hinge letting out a metallic wail that sounded like a pinched tail. Then came the poetry.

"God damnit, fucking piece of dogshit cunt! Feck! Heneghan, get out here!"

I was already moving, trudging around the back of the beast toward my grizzled tour guide in the Church of Hard Knocks.

"See what I see?" he asked.

"Yeah, looks like—"

"Looks like we're stuck deeper than a pecker on prom night, doesn't it?!"

"Yes, sir."

"Cut it with the sir shit. You know what this means, Heneghan?"

Shovel time. That's what it meant.

"I get to dig us out?"

"Thanks for volunteering. I'll be in the truck eating whatever hell is inside our box lunches this time."

"Sounds good, I'll get digging."

Early spring — which in Canada is just winter with trust issues — had turned the hill into a hell broth of slush, mud, and frozen dirt. I dug like a man sentenced to purgatory. Tried the gas. No luck. Dug more. Swore some. Rinse and repeat.

Meanwhile, Liam sat up in the cab like a mud king, watching me and occasionally heckling from the passenger seat.

"Hey, Heneghan, how's things going back there?"

"Oh, y'know... stellar. We're just not going anywhere, ever."

"That's what I figured. Come eat your feckin' box lunch. Let's see what fresh hell they've cooked up today."

I'd been out there long enough to earn a PhD in futility. Some of the other guys drove by — clean trucks, smug grins, and middle fingers. I reciprocated with a mud-caked salute of my own and climbed back in.

"Here," Liam said, handing me a cardboard tomb for my appetite. I opened it to find the usual culinary war crime: stale cheese sandwich, battered apple, granola bar that had clearly lost a fight with a tank tread, and nuts that were probably rations from Korea.

"Ha! Looks like you had the same asshole pack your lunch as I did, Henny."

"Looks that way..."

And yeah, I ate it. All of it. Because hunger doesn't give a shit if your food's depressing.

Just as I'm choking down my third bite of despair, I hear it — a low, diesel growl climbing the hill. Wilmot. My boy. My brother. His rig pulled up beside mine. His instructor, Adamson, rolled the window down and gave me that look — the one friends give when they know you're in deep but they'll still laugh at you anyway.

"Henny, you stuck?"

"Nope. Just parked here to roll in the mud for kicks. Yeah, we're stuck."

"You good? Need a hand?"

"Nah, I'm gonna finish this gourmet nightmare and try again. Thanks, though."

Ignoring me, Wilmot grabbed a shovel and hopped out. I went to join him, but Liam stopped me with a sly grin.

"Heneghan," he said, "Sit. Eat. I'll help the fucker."

He didn't help, of course. He supervised, which in Liam-speak meant coffee, chatting, and offering zero actual assistance. But hey, fifteen minutes later, we were free.

Wilmot led the way, and we rolled toward the main road, eventually pulling into a truck stop by the water to lick our wounds. Those with stomachs stronger than mine finished their lunches. Liam, never one to let a peaceful moment slide, looked over at Chang.

"Chang'er, whad'ya got over there?"

"Uh... roast beef... I think."

"You *think*?! That's the issue right fucking there. Not even knowing what the hell you're eating! I'd like to meet the cock-washer that made these lunches. Shake his goddamn hand. Congratulate him on achieving a doctorate in culinary assholery. Feck!!"

Liam swore with such musical precision, we half considered getting him a mic and sending him on tour.

Weeks passed like that — mud, boxed lunches, dark jokes, and diesel fumes. Eventually, we'd racked up enough hours to earn our military driver's licenses. A license to thrill... and by thrill, I mean grind gears and curse transmissions.

On our last night, we hit up a pub in town. The beer flowed like bad decisions, and for once, we weren't instructors and privates — we were just soldiers, past and future, swapping stories and scars. And then, out of nowhere:

"SHANIA!"

Heads turned. Glasses stopped clinking. It was Liam — sloshed, swaying, and dead serious.

"Sss-shut up and listen! Listen-nnn to me!" he slurred, pointing a trembling finger at all of us.

"You're all getting ready to go on mission, aren't ya?" We nodded. We were bound for Afghanistan, a one-way ticket to a sandbox full of ghosts.

"I've been to bad places. I've done shit things. Married more times than I should'a." He looked each of us in the eye like he was trying to memorize our faces.

"Don't be stupid. SHANIA. You hear me? Don't. Be. Stupid."

It was Shania Twain meets military doctrine. But we got it. He meant: stay alive. Stay smart. Don't be the reason your mother gets a knock on the door.

"You don't be stupid! Keep your eyes open, your mouths shut, and don't volunteer for nothin'! DON'T BE STUPID!! SHANIA!!"

A hand landed on his shoulder, tried to sit him down. He shrugged it off like a man brushing away death.

"SHANIA! You hear me? SHANIA!!"

Eventually, he sat. Took a swig of his brandy like it was a holy sacrament. And the rest of us? We drank too. In silence, in laughter, in fear.

I never saw Liam again. Never heard from any of those instructors. But on July 6, 2008, when the news broke and Wilmot's name was said aloud — KIA in Afghanistan — I knew they'd heard it too. Somewhere, maybe Liam put his coffee down and whispered, *Shania*.

Wilmot wasn't stupid. He was sharp, kind, loyal — everything a good soldier should be. But bombs don't care about any of that. They don't care if you know the lyrics to a catchy Shania song or not.

Since then, I've tried to live by Liam's twisted gospel. I've been stupid a few times, sure — but I remember his voice. That bar. That night.

Thanks, Liam. Wherever you are, I hope the sandwiches are better and the trucks don't stall. And if you're listening...

SHANIA.

# The Pale, Pale Face

Some days I catch it watching me — that old uniform. Midnight blue, stitched with ghosts. It hangs in the closet like a relic from another life. Most people would just see a jacket. Maybe something they'd toss in the goodwill bin next spring. But me? I see chapters. I see blood. I see stories I haven't told anyone. Stories I probably never will.

But maybe, just maybe, I'll tell you this one.

It was a November night, the kind where winter whispers sweet nothings into your ear and the rain feels like it's falling sideways. Late into the shift, my partner Radnor and I got dispatched to a park on the city's northeast side — one of those wooded riverside trails where people pretend they're one with nature until it gets a little too dark and a little too real.

Two hikers flagged us down at the top of the stairs — jittery, bug-eyed, voices cracking like old vinyl. They'd seen something in the trees. A body, maybe. They didn't stick around long enough to confirm. But what really got my attention? They swore it blinked at them.

Right.

So there we were, two allegedly sane adults, descending sixty crooked, moss-slicked stairs into a pitch-black ravine, chasing a ghost story.

You ever walk toward a maybe-dead body that maybe blinked and definitely scared the hell out of two grown humans? You ever do that with your radio dead and your flashlight flickering like it's in on the joke? Let me tell you — it ain't fun.

It took about twelve minutes before I saw her.

She didn't move. Just... stared. Pale as moonlight through cheap whiskey. Her face glowed in the dark — I don't mean metaphorically, I mean it *glowed*. I felt it in my gut, that prehistoric panic that tells you to run. But I couldn't. My feet betrayed me and stayed right where they were. Radnor saw it too.

"Jesus. That is fucking terrifying."

And then she blinked.

Slow. Ghostly. Like death changed its mind halfway through.

"Christ!"

We stood there frozen in that moment — two paramedics, trained professionals, scared stiff by a face in the bush. Eventually, I remembered I had a voice.

"We're paramedics," I said, inching forward. "I'm coming to help you, okay?"

She said nothing. Just blinked again.

I got closer. Long strands of black hair clung to her soaked face. Her shirt was drenched. Jeans stuck to her legs like regret. She was dressed like she'd given up, and maybe she had. Her skin looked like she'd been drained of everything but bitterness.

And then, in a voice barely louder than the wind, she rasped: "Fuck off... Moniyaw."

It's Cree. It means "white man." Usually not a compliment.

Her eyes were... I don't know. Empty? Black. Not metaphorically — actually black. Like she'd looked into the void and it had offered her a loyalty card.

She tried to swing at me, some half-hearted punch powered by fury and frostbite. That's when I saw it — the long, serrated cut running down her arm.

She hadn't just wandered out here to scare hikers. She came to die.

The weather, cold and cruel as it was, had bought her more time than she wanted. Hypothermia slowed the bleeding. The universe had given her one last layover before departure. And she wasn't happy about the delay.

I bandaged her wrist while she spat curses at me. Told me I was dirty, colonial, the enemy. I didn't blame her. Hell, I might've agreed with her if I wasn't so busy trying to keep her alive.

Beside her was the knife. The note. Or what was left of it — rain had made sure the words were lost to time. She hadn't planned on being found.

Radnor ran for help, and I stayed behind — just me and the pale face in the bushes. She cried while I sat beside her, quiet in the dark. I told her I was sorry. That I didn't know her story, but I didn't want her to die. That maybe, just maybe, there was another way. She didn't answer. Just wept into the soil.

We got her out. Took her to the hospital. I didn't say we "saved" her. That word gets tossed around too easily. We didn't save her.

That's the thing no one tells you about this job. Sometimes you show up, do everything right, and it still ends the same. You don't always get to win. Sometimes all you get is a scar, and a uniform that hangs in your closet like a ghost of who you used to be.

I don't wear that uniform anymore.

But I survived. And in the end, that's the happy ending. Not the flashy Hollywood kind — just the quiet, tired, still-here kind. I've built something new. Something soft. Something without sirens and midnight staircases and women dying in the dirt.

And that uniform? It stays in the closet. Wrinkled. Untouched. A museum exhibit for a man I used to be.

May it rest.

May she rest.

And may I keep walking, one step at a time, away from the ghosts and toward something like peace.

Maybe that's all any of us can hope for.

# The CIA Operative with the Broken Ankle

Fifteen years of paramedicine teaches you a lot. Teaches you that people are weird. Pain is weird. And human suffering? Sometimes, hilariously weird. I don't mean that in a "laugh at their misery" way — I'm not a monster — but every so often, amidst the blood and the bile and the broken bones, the universe tosses you a scene so stupid it belongs in a Coen brothers' film.

This is one of those scenes.

Enter: *Doctor Hubert Foster* — the most delightfully deranged South African I've ever met in a hospital. But before we get to the good doctor, let me rewind.

It's night shift. The kind that smells like diesel, regret, and the lingering scent of gas station burritos. Radnor and I are parked on Fifth and Main, doing the usual — trying to pretend we're not freezing to death while daydreaming about our upcoming days off. It's almost

Christmas, which means we're about two bad calls away from seriously considering mall Santa work.

Then dispatch crackles through the speaker, slicing through our idle thoughts like a rusty saw:

***"Medic Three-One, you're heading to the parking lot of Ben's Diner. Police requesting assistance."***

Ben's Diner? At 4:15 a.m.? The place hasn't been open past 7 p.m. since Christ wore short pants. That's already a red flag.

We roll up to a scene out of *Reno 911* — four cruisers scattered across the asphalt like someone rolled for initiative and forgot the grid. Red and blue, lights, cherries and berries I call em, pulse against the black winter sky like a rave no one wanted to attend.

A cop waves us over, points to a guy sprawled out on the ground like he fell out of a slapstick comedy and into a pile of his own bad decisions. Apparently, he was breaking into cars along Birchwood and decided to outrun the cops... on ice. Gravity and karma teamed up for the win — he launched himself into the air like a majestic drunk gazelle and landed ankle-first on the concrete. Ouch.

We approached. His right foot was pointing somewhere in the general direction of "Not Right." Broken. Badly. The kind of break you feel in your own bones just by looking at it.

"Hey, I'm Matthew, we're paramedics," I say, because that's what you say in situations like this.

His reply? Something about my mother and an enthusiastic invitation to a very awkward sexual encounter.

Charming.

Eventually, after some persuasion (and a few less incest-themed retorts), he let us work. We stabilized the mangled mess of bone and ego, pumped him full of happy juice, and loaded him into the back of the rig. His muscles were so tensed from pain that even with meds, we couldn't manipulate the foot. Time for the trauma hospital.

And that's when Doc Foster enters the scene.

Now, Doc Foster... he's a legend. A South African transplant with the bedside manner of a caffeine-deprived raccoon and the charm of a Bond villain. People either loved him or filed complaints about him in triplicate. Me? I thought he was poetry.

We wheel the guy into Room Two. Doc Foster glides in like a man with nowhere better to be and nothing left to prove.

"Breaking into cars, huh?" he booms in his thick accent, looming over the squirming man like a disapproving school principal. "Well, what did we learn?"

The guy blinks, maybe reconsiders his entire life, and says, "I shouldn't run from the cops."

Foster doesn't miss a beat:

"No. You should've worn better shoes."

He pauses.

"Now you've got a broken ankle *and* you're going to jail. And don't even get me started on jail soap."

After attempting to reset the ankle and realizing the guy's pain threshold was about as helpful as a wet match, Foster goes for the Propofol. The good stuff. The kind that knocks you out faster than your ex's text messages used to knock out your self-esteem.

Then, just as he's pushing the meds through the IV, Foster leans in close, like a secret agent at a cocktail party.

"*Hey. Hey, you. How long have you worked for the CIA?*"

Everyone in the room freezes. Even the cop stops writing.

And the guy — this poor, high, broken-footed criminal — mutters:

"...seven years..."

Silence. Total, weightless, absolute silence.

Then, like he just made a three-pointer at the buzzer, Doc Foster snaps the foot back into place and looks up at us like *we're* the weird ones.

"What? I've never had anyone not answer that question. Had a nine-year-old once tell me he'd been undercover for thirteen years. His mom wasn't thrilled either."

Foster tosses his gloves toward the trash like he's Kobe in the final quarter. He misses. Of course. But that, too, is part of his weird, wonderful mythology.

We laughed about it the whole ride back. Made a pact to try the CIA question ourselves someday.

Never did.

Because, honestly, that kind of twisted magic only works when it's wielded by someone like Foster — a little unhinged, a lot brilliant, and totally irreplaceable.

So yeah. That's my story. One of the many scribbled into the seams of my old uniform. The story of a man who ran from cops and ended up with a busted ankle, a CIA confession, and a one-way ticket to jail — all thanks to one eccentric genius with a syringe full of truth serum and a very questionable sense of humor.

And if you're wondering what happened to that guy?

Let's just say he didn't make it back to Langley.

# The Shirt

There are moments in life that sear into your memory like cigarette burns in the leather of your favorite chair — permanent, imperfect, and oddly beautiful in their own screwed-up way. Heartbreak, joy, loss, laughter, trauma, triumph... the usual suspects. We all have them. And like scars, they don't discriminate. Doesn't matter who you are or where you came from — everyone's got a story, even if they're too scared to tell it.

Me? I've got plenty. And this one's about a shirt.

Yeah. A shirt.

Which, let's be honest, sounds ridiculous at first. But stick with me. This isn't a story about cotton and logos — it's about ghosts, guilt, redemption, and a little thing we call hockey.

To start, we need to go back. Spring. Edmonton. The kind of crisp blue sky that makes poets weep and assholes believe in God. I was in uniform then — young, stupid, and hungover enough to convince myself that death by 10k run might be a welcome exit strategy. You see, back then, I served in the army. And that morning? That was a military-grade hangover. One of those "what the hell did I do last night?" situations brought to you by the fine folks at Just One More Drink™.

Our CO was carved out of granite and hatred. He ran like the laws of physics didn't apply to him, and we were expected to keep up — or die trying. Most of us opted for the latter.

After collapsing onto the cold hangar floor like a bag of regrets, I heard the voice of Colin Wilmot, one of the only people who could make that hellscape bearable.

"Henny... stretch it out?"

The guy plopped down beside me, all smirks and sarcasm, like he didn't just spend the last hour defying death. He smelled like aftershave and ambition. Me? I smelled like a brewery. He laughed. I winced. We were friends.

Colin wasn't like me. He was annoyingly fit, purpose-driven, and made kale look cool before Instagram ruined it. But somehow, we clicked. On and off base. We'd play video games, eat charcuterie, scream at Oilers games, and debate which actress deserved to bear our fictional children. (Scarlett Johansson, if you're reading this, my DMs are open.)

He was the kind of guy who'd slap you on the shoulder in the morning just to remind you you're alive. And damn if I didn't need that.

We were gearing up for Afghanistan. The tempo was high. Life was chaotic but good. And then, like all tragic stories that start with laughter, it stopped.

I left the army July 2, 2008. Four days later, Colin left the earth. An IED. Just like that. Boom. Gone.

I got the call from a friend still in. Said it flat. Like ripping off a Band-Aid from a bullet wound. I watched the news later that day —

Colin's face flickering on a TV screen behind the bar I was drinking at. That was the moment the world shifted. Not in some cinematic, slow-mo kind of way. No violins. Just numb silence and stale beer.

I blamed myself. Still do, some days. See, Colin was the alternate. He wasn't supposed to deploy — not unless someone backed out. That someone? Me. My leaving gave him the seat. My absence put him on the plane. It's a cruel math I've never quite made peace with.

Years passed. I kept drinking. Kept running. Not on pavement — from pain. Then came the DUI. Then came the funeral of my mother. Suicide. Then, three years later, my sister — same script, same ending.

And in that ruin, I found writing. Or maybe it found me. Either way, I poured everything I had onto the page — trauma, loss, all of it. A publisher called. A book got made. A piece of my soul got stitched back together.

I wrote about Colin. I gave him a proper eulogy — not with bugles or medals, but with ink and memory. It helped. Not fully, not perfectly, but enough.

The book resonated. People — strangers — reached out. One of them was Phil.

Phil was a medic. Afghanistan vet. Still working the job back home. He wrote me a message that was humble and kind. Told me he had something of mine. Asked for my address. I gave it.

Weeks passed. Then came a snowy afternoon and a surprise package in the mailbox. Inside was a Ziploc bag. Inside the bag? A dirt-stained Edmonton Oilers shirt. With it, a note.

Turns out Phil was deployed to the same FOB as Colin. Assigned to the same bunk. Found the shirt. Colin's shirt. Left behind in the chaos of war, it had survived. And Phil, knowing what it meant, took it home. Carried it with him for years, trying to find where it belonged. That place, it turns out, was with me.

On December 16th, 2021 — Colin came home for Christmas.

So yeah... this shirt? It's not just a shirt. It's a relic. A fragment. A whisper from a better man who deserved more time. And in a way, it brought two broken souls together — me and Phil. Brothers now. Bound by memory, loss... and hockey.

Let's go, Oilers.

Let's go.

(I know... I said I was a Sens fan — and I am. But c'mon; after a story like this, how do you *not* cheer for the Oil?)

# Ghosts in the Chair

Father's Day. That charming, complicated little bastard of a holiday. The one with all the ties no one asked for and the burnt toast breakfast delivered by sticky fingers and wide eyes — unless you're like me. Then it's something else entirely.

See, I didn't grow up with a dad. Not in the Hallmark sense. No sage advice, no catch in the backyard, no quiet wisdom passed down from the driver's seat. Just absence. A void in the shape of a man. The kind of space that echoes louder than words.

It wasn't until I joined the army that I met real fathers. Guys who could break you in half with their pinky finger during a ruck march and then melt into mush when their kid hands them a stick-figure simulacrum of *dad's* likeness. I saw that on graduation day—tough-as-nails soldiers cracking like glass when their sons and daughters ran into their arms. Watching them, it clicked. All that grit and grind, all those sleepless nights and blistered feet—they weren't doing it just for the flag. They were doing it for their kids. For love. For legacy.

And then there was me. Alone. No father to salute me. No little one running into my arms. Just standing there like a ghost with rank stitched on my chest.

Fast forward a few years. I'm a paramedic now, trading fatigues for navy blues and Kevlar for latex gloves. Different war, same chaos. I get a call—man down, unresponsive, slumped in a chair. We roll up, lights flashing, but it's already too late. He's gone. Just... gone. Peaceful, in a chair surrounded by books and scattered memories. He looked like someone who once had answers.

The wife makes the call. Her son shows up. Grown man, built like a brick wall, but the second he sees the body in the chair, he crumbles. Shatters. He drops to his knees, sobbing in a voice only little boys use when they lose their hero.

I stood in the doorway, a silent witness to a scene I've seen more times than I care to count—grief unfolding in real-time. Real, raw, and ruthless. He called him "Dad" in a way that made me jealous. Made me ache.

That job left a mark on me. Not because of the death. That's just Tuesday. But because I realized, again, that I never had what that man in the doorway just lost.

But here's the twist... I'm not bitter anymore. Not like I used to be. Because in my life now, I'm surrounded by men who get it. Dads who show up, who laugh, who lead by example, who love without ego. They've become my beacons of fatherhood. They've helped me redefine the word *father*.

So, to the real dads out there—the ones who give a damn, who hug tight, who teach and try and show up even when it's hard—this one's for you. You're the ones keeping the torches lit for guys like me. You're writing new definitions for a word that once only meant pain.

Happy Father's Day. You beautiful, stubborn, soft-hearted bastards.

Keep carrying the flame. Some of us are still learning how to hold it.

# The Uniform That Killed the Man

January. The world's most ironic fresh start.

A month draped in gym memberships, well-intentioned resolutions, and overpriced planners. A month people swear by as their chance to become someone new, while most of us are still dragging around the ghosts of who we were last December. For me, January doesn't taste like renewal — it tastes like static in a snow globe. It sounds like silence after the tone drops. It feels like grief that never quite melts with the snow.

It feels like Greg.

I met Greg Turner in 2007. I was still a medic in the Canadian Armed Forces — a kid in a uniform, trying to stitch meaning into chaos and hide the imposter syndrome under well-polished boots. We were doing a ride-along program to sharpen our trauma skills, tossed into the belly of the urban beast: downtown Edmonton. That's where I met Greg — a man built like a bouncer but with the soul of a librarian. Voice like rolling thunder, kindness like warm coffee on a frostbitten morning.

He didn't strut. He didn't bluster. He *was*. Solid. Stoic. Serene.

He told me what he expected from me on day one — then turned and asked if I wanted a coffee. That was Greg. Direct, decent, and decaffeinated compassion in human form. He showed me the ropes without turning them into a noose. When I fumbled, he didn't roll his eyes — he rolled up his sleeves. The guy was a masterclass in pre-hospital care, and I knew from hour one: *this is the kind of medic I want to be.*

A year later, I traded in my military uniform for paramedic blues, and like some cosmic joke wrapped in municipal budgeting, I ended up working in the same service I'd trained with. I was in the back of the rig doing stock count when I heard that unmistakable voice — Greg. I stepped out like a kid hoping to be noticed at a high school reunion.

"You've got a different uniform than last time I saw ya," he said.

"Yes, sir."

"Looks good on ya."

Coming from Greg? That was like getting knighted. The man didn't dole out compliments unless they were earned. And from time to time, I had the privilege of working alongside him. Watching him work was like watching Ed Sheeran write lyrics, like watching a surgeon dance. He knew the rhythm of a call — the unspoken tempo of chaos. He wasn't just good at his job. He *was* his job — the kind of guy who didn't just patch people up but left them better for having met him.

I asked him once, during one of those godawful 14-hour shifts, if he still loved it. You know — the job. The grind. The trauma parade. The never-ending shift that is being a paramedic.

His reply was as steady as the man: "I do. This never feels like a job. I love it."

Eleven words. Tattooed into my brain. He meant them, too.

And then, January 26, 2015, Greg died in the back of an ambulance. Suicide.

The place he gave his life to — the city, the service, the streets — became the place that took it back.

This is the part no one puts in the recruitment brochures. The part no one tells you in orientation. That the uniform doesn't always come off when you clock out. That the trauma you soak in eventually stains your soul. You memorize death like a playlist — apartment 4B, the overdose; 12A, the suicide; a jumper at the bridge; a baby who didn't make it. The city becomes a graveyard you can't stop driving through.

Greg was stronger than most. He held the line longer than many. He smiled when others screamed. But the horror show eventually finds us all. It worms its way into our off days, our dreams, our coffee cups. Greg didn't die because he was weak. He died because he was *human* in an inhuman system. And he fought longer than anyone should've had to.

I think about him every January. Every time the snow settles and the world goes quiet, I hear his voice. I see that tired grin. I remember the coffee, the patience, the mentorship. I remember the man. Not the job title. Not the tragedy. *The man.*

"So that others may live" — that's the creed we throw around like a slogan. But sometimes, tragically, it's a prophecy.

Greg Turner lived it. And Greg Turner died by it.

Rest easy, brother. You are missed more than these words can hold. Thank you for the lessons, the laughter, and the kindness. Thank you for teaching me what the job *could* be — and for showing me that the greatest medics aren't the loudest or the fastest... they're the ones who care, even when it breaks them.

P.S. The next coffee's on me. But don't expect me to drink it without a tear.

# The Day Music Didn't Play

I was twenty-five the day the war finally reached me — not with bullets or sand, but in whiskey and silence. May 6th, 2008. Spring was in bloom, sure, but for me, it may as well have been winter in a graveyard. Everything felt dead.

The bar smelled like old decisions and cheaper regrets. One of those dim little places that pretends to be cozy but really just hosts the ghosts of men who never quite made it home. I found the darkest booth I could. Far corner, beneath a tired neon Molson sign flickering like it was trying to die in peace. My drink sat in front of me, trembling, not because of my hand — but because of everything it knew.

Half a world away, a flag was folded into sharp military corners. A mother screamed. A rifle cracked three times in final punctuation. Michael was gone. And I was here. Sipping bourbon, pretending it helped.

His face was on the screen above the bar. The TV was muted, but the volume of that moment screamed louder than anything I've ever heard. “Canadian soldier killed in Afghanistan,” the ticker said — like he was some stock that just took a dip. His name, his face, condensed into pixels and chyron tape.

Cpl. Michael Starker. My friend. My brother.

I hated that bar for not stopping. Hated the bartender for pouring drinks like nothing had changed. Hated the jukebox for having the audacity to keep playing Red Hot Chili Peppers. Hated the people for laughing — clinking glasses as though the earth hadn’t just lost something irreplaceable. They didn’t know. They couldn’t. But I hated them anyway.

The whiskey didn’t taste like absolution. It tasted like cowardice. Like I should’ve been there — in uniform, in the dirt, with him. But I wasn’t. I was nestled safely within Canada, playing at pretending to put some good in the world dressed in the uniform of a paramedic. Trying to fake being some stable version of myself. A version without the nightmares. The one who hadn’t yet met the boy with no face or held the hand of the dying.

And there I sat. In some forgettable dive, trying to apologize to a ghost who’d never hear it.

Two years before that, we lost Eykelenboom — “Boomer.” First medic to fall since Korea. I thought that was the bottom. Turns out, the elevator kept going.

I blinked, and there was Michael. Sand in his boots. A quiet stare that could crack granite. That voice — sharp, smart-assed, and wise beyond its years — echoing between the ice machine and the clack of pool balls. I saw him. I heard him. And then I didn’t.

I raised my glass. Not in toast. Not in grief. Maybe in shame. Maybe just to keep my hands busy.

You taught me more than you'll ever know, brother. Dignity. Discipline. The kind of self-respect you can't fake. I haven't always lived up to those lessons, but I carry them — the way I carry you.

Every year, this date comes around. And every year, I look out the window like a fool, hoping to see you walking up the driveway, late as ever, calling me a "lazy civvy piece of shit." But the driveway stays empty. And I stay haunted.

Rest easy, Michael. You were better than most. Braver than all. And you were my friend.

I'll see you again. If there's any justice in the universe, I'll see you again.

# The Pizza Was Hot. He Wasn't

Did you know that May 18th to the 25th is considered Paramedic Services Week?

It's okay if you didn't. I didn't either — at least not until I found myself wearing navy blue and chasing sirens into the worst days of people's lives. Before that, I probably lumped paramedics into the same vague category as most folks do: Ambulance drivers. EMT guys. Hospital people.

It started as EMS (Emergency Medical Services) Week back in 1974, a government gesture that flared up and burned out just as fast. It vanished like a good idea in a boardroom full of budget cuts. It wasn't until 1992, when the American College of Emergency Physicians gave it mouth-to-mouth, that it came back to life. Since then, one week in May gets carved out to nod in the direction of paramedics. A cordial acknowledgment to the ones who tow the line between life and death.

Now, if you're expecting a story with fireworks and hero shots, you're going to be disappointed. But if you'll let me, I'll tell you a true one. A day I still carry around in the beat-up pockets of memory.

We were dispatched to a call for a cardiac arrest. Middle-aged male. Public location. No further details.

When we got there, he was slumped in the passenger seat of his wife's modest four-door sedan. Face grey. Breath gone. She was screaming — but not the kind of scream you hear in movies. Hers was hollow and cracking, like a person trying to keep themselves from vanishing. Movies never quite get the screams right. No matter how talented the actor or actress. At the end of the day, they are acting — these people are not.

We pulled him out. Did everything we were trained to do. Compressions. Drugs. Shocks... Hope. We worked on him as hard as we could on the way to the hospital. My partner and I were in the back, and a police officer drove the rig for us. Always an adventure as police are used to driving with a little more vigor and agility. Getting thrown around while trying to insert needles, breathing tubes, and administer time-sensitive medication isn't your typical Tuesday — unless you're a paramedic. In which case... it can be.

When we got to the hospital downtown, we maneuvered the man lain on our stretcher down corridors, past other patients stacked like boxes along the pastel hallways in some forgotten warehouse of the damned. You can feel the inquisition of peering eyes staple themselves to the back of your neck as you roll by. But your busy, so you pay it no mind, other than to feel it.

We got him into a trauma room and handed over care while explaining our interventions enroute.

But that day, hope and skill wasn't enough.

A doctor took over. Called it. Just like that. And then the body — no longer a person — was covered by a thin characterless sheet and all the bustle and all the noise was stilled. He was dead and we were tired.

Me? I was tired of the dead. I'd been on a bad stint as of late. Bestowed the moniker of being a "black cloud" by my partners. Meaning that those working with me were reluctant to do so, because we were sure to get some big calls. Or sad ones. A lot of sad ones.

As I typed up our paperwork, retelling the story of death, a doc came around and handed out slices of pizza. A small kindness for the medics still jammed in the hallway with patients on stretchers and IVs hanging from portable poles. No real place to sit. No real time to process. Just a hallway and another call waiting. This is commonplace in our hospitals. Hallways and the dead coexisting, sometimes as one, and some poor medic trying to finish paperwork and inhale any bit of food they can before the next run.

I took the slice. It smelled good — like grease and basil and the perfect un petit peu of distraction. I was about to bite in when I saw her. The wife. The widow.

She'd just come through the ER doors. Her face was blotchy and wet. Eyes red. The kind of pain that no mirror should ever reflect back at you. The kind that only comes from death. She saw me and bounded toward me.

"Where is he? Where is my husband?" She clutched onto my arm, shaking it, causing pepperoni and onion to flee and fall to the floor.

"Ma'am..." I gestured for her to follow me to the quiet room. A small room with a heavy door where bad news is delivered to those left behind. "Ma'am — we did everything that we could, but I am so sorry — your husband has passed away. He's gone."

I delivered the death notification with a doomed slice of pizza still held precarious in my hand.

I wasn't hungry anymore.

I walked over to the trash can and let it fall into the black.

It wasn't guilt, exactly. It wasn't even sadness. It was something quieter. Heavier. Like the realization that while I got to move on to the next call, she'd be stuck in this one for the rest of her life. That's a hard one to grapple with. But that notion is one I confronted many times throughout my career as a medic.

That's the part of this job no one really tells you about. How can they? Death makes perfect sense, but the absence of what it leaves behind doesn't. And that's just heartbreaking.

We — paramedics — don't get to pause. We don't get to process a lot of the time. There's no halftime in the lives of strangers. You hand in your paperwork, wipe your hands with sanitizer, and get back in the truck. You clear from the hospital, and the radio chirps again. Another call. Another scene. Another person whose world is about to change forever.

This is the job. To face inhumanity with such repetition, that speaking about it no longer seems viable. You just show up and do the best you can. Until you can't.

I was diagnosed with PTSD in 2017. I have never returned to work. After countless hours in therapists' chairs, occupational stress injury clinics, it was decided that I was unfit to return. My uniform now hangs in the shadows of my closet. My nametag collects dust. Yet, each time I go to pick it up, it's still weighted by the heft of memory and loss.

Paramedics aren't superheroes. We're just people. Tired, often hungry, sometimes sullen. We carry trauma in invisible duffel bags and hope it doesn't burst open on a Tuesday.

So, this Paramedic Services Week, if you know one — thank them. And if you don't, that's okay too. Just remember that when you hear the wail of a siren, someone's sprinting toward pain all while carrying their own.

This week, I will pause to reflect. To Remember.

To those I have loved, lost and worked alongside...

I will remember you.

This week.

Every week.

# The One That Got Away

I didn't know what to say. Every word that tiptoed to the edge of my tongue felt cheap, flimsy — like handing someone a paper umbrella in a thunderstorm. So I said nothing. Just sat in the thick silence with Radnor, both of us crushed beneath the bloated weight of disappointment. The night air hung around us like a sweat-soaked blanket. A chorus of bored crickets carried on their symphony of indifference as Radnor knelt there, staring at the pavement like it had personally let him down.

Eventually, he looked up. Sorrow in his eyes. I met it with a look that said, "Yeah... same." He stood, walked back to the ambulance, opened the rust-hinged door with all the grace of a dying banshee, and slammed it shut. Silence again. Until:

"Matty..." he said.

"Yeah, buddy..." I replied, just above a whisper.

"We lost him. He's gone... he's definitely gone."

I didn't say anything. Just let my shoulders speak for me. They sagged in defeat.

But let's rewind. Before the heartbreak, before the missed opportunity, before the raccoon-sized hole was carved into our egos — let's start at the beginning.

It was a hot August night. Sticky, thick air. One of those evenings where even the moon looked like it needed a shower. Radnor and I were paired for a night tour — 8 p.m. to 8 a.m. — the graveyard shift, or as we liked to call it, "The Vampire Bus." My regular partner was off nursing a cold, and Radnor's was off nursing a margarita on vacation. So it was just us, two battle-weary medics with too many miles and not enough patience.

We kicked things off by washing the rig. Not because we're saints, but because we had time — and clean trucks made for better first impressions when rolling up on a mess. There were jokes, a splash war, maybe a few middle fingers. Then, duty called.

First call: two college girls experimenting with pot and paranoia in a motel that smelled like ashtrays and regret. Room 302. The elevator ride up was like a death-defying game of Will These Cables Hold? Spoiler: they did. Barely.

We knocked. Got some panicked voices behind the door and a request for "paramedical badges," which, of course, don't exist. Radnor, being the poet he is, let them know, "All we get is back pain and a shitty pension." He wasn't wrong.

Inside, two girls stared at us like we'd arrived from Mount Olympus. One of them hugged Radnor like he was the second coming of Beyoncé. The diagnosis? First-time stoners. No vitals, no transport, no drama — just a craving for Doritos. Radnor even recommended Cool Ranch. Always the professional.

We laughed our way back to the rig, only to be met by Todd — shift supervisor and bureaucratic buzzkill. Todd was the kind of guy who could make a coffee order feel like a performance review. His voice was Pee-wee Herman meets a vacuum cleaner. His latest crisis? A raccoon had allegedly broken into the station, stolen his lunch, and shit on the bay floor. Not necessarily in that order.

Now, to be fair, Todd's lunch was an egg salad sandwich — a culinary crime in its own right. But the man was livid. Swore vengeance against raccoons everywhere. Radnor and I? We couldn't stop laughing. Until we did.

Because later that night, driving through the heat with the windows down and the AC busted, I saw something. A flicker of movement by a bush near a hydrant. I told Radnor to stop. Spotlighted the bastard like we were filming Cops: Woodland Edition. And there it was — the raccoon. The raccoon. Beady-eyed and brazen, probably still nursing Todd's sandwich.

Radnor was ready. Slid out of the rig like a SEAL on recon. Every step precise. Quiet. Perfect. We were seconds away from greatness — from trapping the little bastard and releasing him in Todd's SUV like the twisted urban legends we were born to be.

And then... the voice.

"Mr. Heneghan, or should I say, Mr. Laughy Pants, Echo-One?!"

Todd.

Of course it was Todd.

He'd crept up like a fart in a funeral and blasted any hope we had of catching our furry fugitive. Radnor fell to his knees like he'd just watched the love of his life walk out the door. The raccoon bolted, flipping us the metaphorical middle claw as he disappeared into the night.

Todd, unaware of the emotional carnage he'd just caused, offered a smug chuckle and drove off like he'd just won something.

We never caught that raccoon. And Todd kept bringing those egg salad sandwiches to work, microwaving them like a war crime in progress. But every time Radnor and I passed each other in the hospital halls or crossed paths on the road, our eyes would meet and say it all:

We almost had him.

Some wounds never heal. Some legends never die. And some raccoons just know how to make a clean getaway.

# Midnights Are Not So Quiet

I stood over him like a busted statue—weather-worn, chipped, and tired. There wasn't a damn thing I could do. Not for him. Not for her.

The woman—his wife—was unraveling right there in front of me, grief pouring out of her in guttural wails. She beat her fists against my chest like I'd personally betrayed her. Maybe I had. Maybe we both knew it. The Kevlar vest absorbed the blows, left her with nothing but bruised hands and a shattered world.

Her son stepped in, quietly prying her off me with the tenderness of someone who'd spent a lifetime playing peacekeeper. He looked at me, just a small nod. I gave him one back. A wordless exchange between two men watching the same moment slip away.

I'd been around death plenty by then. Too much. You start to catalog it—not out of morbid curiosity, but as a way to manage it. File it away. Keep it clinical so it doesn't crawl inside and fester. But it still does. It always does.

The man on the floor? He was already halfway gone before we got there. Cancer had hollowed him out. Skin like wax paper stretched over bone. He looked like a chalk sketch of a human being. The kind of body that tells you the soul's already packed its bags.

It was just past midnight, cold enough outside to make the world feel brittle. The call came in as a collapse. The man had gotten up to use the washroom and dropped like a marionette with the strings cut.

I remember the sound of snow underfoot as we approached the house. That soft, dry crunch of winter; the last peaceful thing I'd hear that night. Funny how you remember things like that. You cling to them like driftwood.

Inside, the house was dim. One long hallway. One light on — the bathroom at the end. A man, maybe late thirties, was kneeling in the doorway, holding up a body that clearly wasn't helping him. His voice cracked the air.

"Help me, please. He's not breathing. I can't move him."

I dropped the trauma bag, stepped into the light. That's when I saw him... the father. Naked except for a pair of briefs, collapsed halfway on the toilet, twisted like a figure left mid-dance. He was thin in the kind of way that only cancer and time can manage. His ribs looked like piano keys under bruised parchment.

And then the smell hit. The unmistakable, sobering stench of death. He'd soiled himself. It happens. The body forgets its dignity when the soul starts walking toward the exit.

We moved him — me on the top half, the son on the legs. Set him down on a patch of hallway floor. The bathroom light spilled out behind us, and my partner flicked on his flashlight. That thin beam cut through the dark, while the red-and-white strobes from our truck outside danced across the walls like ghosts trying to make themselves seen.

"Ma'am," my partner said gently, "do you have a Do Not Resuscitate order for your husband?"

She didn't answer. Didn't blink. Her grief had taken the wheel.

The son looked up. "Yes. We do."

"Can you get it?"

That's when she broke. "Don't you dare," she hissed. "Don't you damn well dare."

The son didn't flinch. He got up, walked off, and came back with a green folder. Classic hospital fare. Stickered, folded, and full of final wishes. Inside: a document clear as glass. No CPR. No drugs. No tube. Nothing.

Her voice turned to a low growl. She begged us. Ordered us. Screamed at us to help him. But we couldn't. Legally, ethically, humanly — we were bound to do nothing. So we stood there like four statues in a museum of grief, watching a man hiccup his way out of life.

Every time his chest convulsed with another agonal breath, she looked at me. Eyes full of desperation. Rage. Pleading. I couldn't look away, but I couldn't give her what she wanted, either. I just shook my head, quietly, slowly. No.

I hear her scream sometimes. Still. It shows up just as I'm about to fall asleep, like some kind of cruel soundtrack queued up by my subconscious. It slices through the stillness, and suddenly I'm wide-eyed and thirteen years deep in memory.

Stuff like this is why I was three fingers deep in whiskey for more then a decade of my life.

The job teaches you a lot. Teaches you how to carry weight. Teaches you how to smile at strangers while your soul bleeds in private. But it doesn't teach you how to forget. It doesn't teach you how to sleep through screams that aren't there.

Nights like this, I sit up instead. Try to remind myself that I did everything I was allowed to. That honoring a man's final wish is also a kind of saving. That sometimes doing nothing is the most ethical thing you can do. But that's a hard pill to swallow when someone's punching your chest and calling you a monster.

I don't hate her for it. Not even a little. She loved him. And love, in its loudest moments, doesn't give a damn about green folders or end-of-life care plans. Love just wants another minute.

But time doesn't trade in minutes. Time takes what it's owed and leaves you holding the receipt.

So here I am. Awake again. Heart racing. Replay stuck on loop.

And like always, I try to remind myself: this too shall pass. Maybe not tonight. Maybe not for a while. But eventually.

Nothing is permanent. Not life. Not sorrow. None of it. So this too shall pass.

"No matter how many times you fail, it does not mean you cannot succeed."

— Matthew Heneghan

# MUSINGS ABOUT LIFE'S LITTLE MOMENTS

# Stillness and Steam

I was in my backyard this morning. The grass was wet, not in that sexy summer-rain kind of way, but in that "you'll regret wearing socks" kind of way. The sun was dragging itself up from behind the mountains like a hungover prizefighter answering the bell. Pine trees lit up like they'd been brushed with melted caramel. God's own Instagram filter.

The dogs were being idiots in the best way. Paws kicking up dew, tails wagging like windshield wipers on a monsoon day. My tea sat beside me, steam coiling upward like it had something important to say but was too shy to speak. And for once, I wasn't thinking about what I needed to fix, or finish, or run from. I just... sat.

Sheena and I are working on this yard. It's a bit of a fixer-upper — kind of like me. There's a patch of dirt that one day will be a pool, and just outside the door, I imagined the quiet gurgle of a hot tub that doesn't exist yet, but already feels like an old friend.

None of that's happened yet, of course. But other things have. Big things. Life things. Somehow, despite a head full of ghosts and a résumé full of blood and sirens, I've found myself here. With peace. With love. With plans.

And it hit me — not like a bolt of lightning or a punch to the gut — but like warm sunlight on a cold back. Gratitude. Real, holy-shit-I'm-still-here gratitude.

The smile came before I realized I was smiling. That's how you know it's real.

I thought about where I've been. Darker places. Colder mornings. Mornings that didn't come because I hadn't gone to sleep yet. Back then, serenity was a stranger I wouldn't have recognized even if she sat across from me on the bus and slapped me with a daisy.

Even now, part of me wonders if I deserve this life. This quiet. This cup of tea that isn't spiked. But the people around me — the real ones, the ones who stayed — they seem to think I do. And maybe, just maybe, I believe them. Enough to keep going. Enough to stay.

By the time my mind wandered back, the sun had fully clocked in for the day. The birds started up — tiny lunatics with feathers and a soundtrack to match. The dew dried, the shadows retreated, and the world looked brand new again.

You know, this life — it's a ridiculous thing. Loud, tragic, messy, miraculous. And if you don't slow the hell down once in a while, you'll miss the whole damn point.

But not this morning.

This morning, I was here. Really here. No scripts, no filters, no filters on the filters. Just me, the dogs, a cup of tea, and the honest-to-God feeling that maybe everything doesn't suck all the time. Maybe it never did. Maybe I just stopped noticing.

So, here's what I hope for you: a minute. Just one. A moment where the noise stops, the light hits just right, and your tea — or your coffee, or whatever the hell you're into — is hot, not lukewarm.

As Shakespeare said — and man, that guy could write — "In peace, there's nothing so becomes a man as modest stillness and humility."

Stillness and humility. Two things that don't cost a dime but might just save your soul.

Anyway... that was my Tuesday morning.

How was yours?

# THE WHARF

There's a place I go when the world gets too loud. It doesn't scream for attention. It just is — tucked away like a well-kept secret next to the lake, as if God himself decided to keep one little slice of serenity untouched. The grass sways like it's dancing with the wind, and unless you're really looking — I mean, really looking — you'd miss it.

They call it The Wharf.

Simple name. Quiet place. But for me, it was never just a wooden walkway curling out into the Shuswap. It was more like a time machine for the broken-hearted. I found it as a kid, back when everything felt like it was on fire. Home wasn't exactly a Disney flick. More like a Tarantino movie with less blood and way more awkward silences. But this place... this place whispered instead of yelled.

From the first time I saw it, something stirred in my chest — not quite love, but definitely lust. The kind of lust that doesn't fade. I stood at the end of that weathered plank trail and stared out at mountains and water that looked like they were still deciding which one got to be more beautiful.

And if you time it right, just as the sun clocks out for the day, you get this view. A golden glaze spills across the trees like honey on warm bread. The sky starts undressing slowly — slipping into pastels and bruised purples, blushing pinks. It's not heaven, but it's close enough to fool a guy who doesn't believe in it.

This place — this creaky, splintered, wonderful little wharf — made me feel something. As a boy, it gave me magic. As a man, it gives me something even rarer: peace.

Flash forward to 2019, two years after my mother decided the fight was over. Suicide. That word still tastes like metal in my mouth. I stood on that wharf again, this time under a sky so grey it made ash look optimistic. Snowflakes wandered their way down to the lake like they weren't in a rush to get anywhere. I had a friend with me, but he read the room — or the silence, rather — and gave me space.

We never had a proper funeral. My family's kind of like a dropped jigsaw puzzle — fragmented as hell and missing a few corners. Grief tends to do that. So that morning, I held my own little ceremony. Just me, the lake, and some memories I wasn't sure I could still remember right.

I ran my hand along the railing. Felt every groove like braille written by time. And then, the movie started — my life on shuffle. I saw my mom smile, which she didn't do nearly enough. I saw myself in high school, kidnapped by a pack of well-meaning sadists — the senior girls — who stuffed us into dresses for the graduation gag photo. My mom was in on it, of course. She held the door open. Laughing.

Proud.

Wicked.

And in the background of that photo? The wharf. Always the wharf. Watching quietly. Never judging.

When the mental slideshow stopped playing, I was crying. Quietly. The kind of crying that sneaks up on you and slaps you across the face with everything you thought you'd buried. But in that moment, I remembered her not as the woman broken by disease or depression — but as the woman who laughed. Who lived.

And for the first time in two years, I let her go. I whispered a messy little eulogy — "thank you, I love you, forever, always..." — and the wharf didn't say anything. It just held me. Like it always had.

So yeah... there's this place. A place that doesn't beg to be found but should be. A place where magic still dares to exist. It's not flashy. It's not famous. But it's everything.

It's called The Wharf.

And it's waiting.

If you're interested, head to Salmon Arm B.C. and check it out for yourself. Toss it a thought or two. It'll be kind. I promise.

# Need Mum Kind of Moment

I thought of you today.

One of those "need mom" kind of moments. You know the kind — where the weight of the world is a little too heavy, the silence in the room a little too loud, and everything you thought you had figured out suddenly feels like a lie you told yourself to sleep at night.

You're gone. Like, really gone. Not in the poetic, "off to a better place" kind of way — but gone-gone. No forwarding address. No return calls. Just... nothing. And even now, it doesn't compute. My brain gets it, but my heart? Still waiting for your laugh to echo through a room it hasn't touched in years.

I know all the grief bumper stickers. I've read the Hallmark-card theology. "She lives on in you." "She's always with you." "Just think of her and she's there." And my personal favorite: "She's all around you."

Yeah, well, if she's all around me, maybe she could show up with a hug and a cup of tea. Maybe she could knock some sense into me like she used to — without ever raising her voice. Maybe she could just be here.

But she's not. And those platitudes — they're like paper towels trying to mop up a flood. Nice try, but grief has a way of overflowing everything.

Some days it feels like I'm standing on the shore of a life I used to know, watching memories drift out past the horizon like ships with no sails. I throw rocks into the water hoping to make a dent, to bring something back. But all I get are ripples that vanish before they reach my feet.

And I get it — this is life now. The adult in me has bills to pay, people to show up for, stories to write. But the kid? The one you used to read to, the one who used to cry quietly because he didn't want to worry you? That kid still misses his mum. Desperately.

When I close my eyes, I see you as you were — not the sick, fading version, but the real you. Smiling. Mischievous. Strong. And when I open them, the world rushes in like a cold slap to the face, and your image gets washed away in the noise. Some days, blinking is the most painful thing I do.

You and I, we talked about suicide more than most mothers and sons probably do. It came with the job, with the uniform. I knew the stats. Knew the calls. Knew the weight. But I never thought I'd get your name on the list. Not you. Not my mum.

I wish you'd called me that night. I wish you'd told me the darkness was creeping in. I would've fought it for you. I would've sat with it. With you. But instead, I talk to ghosts. Yours mostly.

So yeah... I thought of you today. In that "need mom" kind of way.

And if you are all around me... I hope you heard.

# Hi, I'm Yours

The morning started the way so many of mine do — breathless, panicked, tangled in sheets and shadows. PTSD's way of saying good morning, sunshine. Hotel rooms are the worst. No matter how many stars you slap on the brochure, unfamiliar ceilings don't care about your trauma. They echo it. Amplify it. Remind you that you're not at home, not really anywhere, just floating in a borrowed space with ghosts that never check out.

Eric, a dear friend of mine, was snoring in the other bed — the kind of deep, innocent sleep that belongs to men who haven't seen too much. Or maybe just men who've managed to bury it better. I didn't wake him. That was my one small victory of the hour.

I reached for my nightmare bag — yeah, that's a thing — a curated kit of sensory lifelines designed to yank me back from the hellscapes behind my eyelids. There's a teddy in there. Ted, like the movie. A foul-mouthed little bastard from Boston. He's a one-to-one replica and, frankly, a better therapist than many I've met. I take a sick kind of pleasure in knowing that hotel staff will see him neatly placed on the bed and wonder what the hell two grown men were up to in this room. Let 'em wonder.

We were in Salmon Arm — my hometown. A picturesque little place tucked between forested mountains and childhood trauma. I had a book signing later that morning, hence the hotel. And the insomnia. And the nerves.

Salmon Arm. Even the name sounds like a half-forgotten story you'd tell drunk around a fire. But to me, it's sacred ground. Last place my mum was alive. I guess that's enough to make any place feel like home, even if all it has left is echoes.

The signing was a big deal. My publisher made it happen. November 9, 2019. My name in the paper. A table stacked with my memoir. It was the closest I'd ever come to fame, and the only place that would ever mean anything to feel it in.

I couldn't sleep, so Eric woke up too — solidarity by insomnia. We showered, separately of course, dressed, and went to get breakfast. I took him to the wharf, that long stretch of wood that juts out into the lake like it's trying to escape town. I used to sit there as a kid, wondering if life got easier or just weirder. Turns out it's both.

The clouds hung low like the universe was having second thoughts. I barely touched my breakfast. Anxiety tends to dull the appetite — even for a greasy sausage and egger. I kept wondering if anyone would show up at the bookstore. Or worse, if only people who knew me would.

But people did show. In waves, even. I signed books until my hand cramped. I smiled until my face felt like it might betray me. And then, amid a lull, she walked in.

Not just her — Shannon, an old classmate. But standing beside her was someone else. Someone electric. Someone with the kind of smile that sends neurons into crisis. Someone who turned out to be

Sheena — a girl I supposedly went to school with and somehow failed to remember. But there's remembering, and then there's seeing. And now, I couldn't look away.

We talked. She smiled. I malfunctioned. Something about her voice made my bones settle. My synapses slowed. And when they left, I watched the taillights like a kid watches the end of summer.

Days later, I was back in Toronto, sipping tea and pretending to be calm. My phone buzzed. It was her. She'd read my book — cover to cover in a single day. Said it made her cry. Said she didn't know how much pain I'd been hiding behind a smile.

We never stopped talking after that.

Turns out, she wasn't married. Not anymore. As it happened to be, life had roughed her up too. We swapped scars, stories, and slow-growing hope. And now, she's the first thought in my morning and the last one at night.

In writing that book — filled with my ghosts, regrets, and half-buried truths — I thought I was giving something to the world. But really, I was making my way home. One word at a time. And at the end of that road, standing just off to the left, was a woman named Sheena — poetry in a Tim Hortons parking lot.

This October, I'm leaving Toronto. For good. I'm going home. Not just to the town, but to her. Because every story has a first line, and mine was:

"Hi... I'm Matthew."

And if I'm lucky, the last one will be:

"Baby... I'm yours."

# Wish I May, Wish I Might

I spent last night whispering my secrets to the stars. Just me, a late-night coffee I wasn't supposed to have, and the kind of night sky that makes you feel microscopic — like God's thumbprint pressed against your chest. I figured if I stood there long enough, soaking in the cosmic silence, something would shift. Some celestial telegram would fall into my lap with the answers I've been begging for since the first-time life kicked me in the teeth.

Spoiler alert: it didn't.

The universe, in all its sparkly indifference, had nothing for me. No postcards from the beyond. No epiphanies. No closure. Just a man standing in the cold, quietly unraveling. I stood there with one wish caught in my throat — to be normal. Whatever the hell that means.

But I know what it means to me. It means not jumping at shadows in the cereal aisle. Not tasting copper in the back of my throat every time a red-light blinks in the periphery. It means sitting at a damn backyard party with my girlfriend and not morphing into a shell of myself because some kid has light-up sneakers that remind me of the strobe on a cruiser the night Pumpkin Man died.

Yeah. Normal. I've been wishing on stars like that since I was ten. All those stars, all that hope, and I still ended up here — a freak with a therapist on speed dial and a brain like a haunted house with no exits.

So, about that party...

Sheena — that's my girl — invites me to meet her inner circle. Backyard soirée, kids running wild, fairy lights strung up like it's a Hallmark movie. This is her world. Her safe place. And I, being the brooding romantic I am, wanted to be part of it. To show them that the broken guy in the corner is more than just jagged edges.

I tried. Christ, I tried.

But as soon as we pull into the driveway, it starts. Kids screaming. Laughter ricocheting like gunfire. Smells, sounds, lights — all of it slamming into me like a freight train full of bad memories. I'm scanning the backyard like a combat zone, heart thumping, breath shallow.

And then, introductions. Sweet, well-meaning people with real lives and mortgages and Pinterest boards. Meagan — pretty blonde, nice voice. But somewhere between hello and small talk, her face starts to dissolve. And in its place, the dead girl. You know the one, if you've read the book. She shows up uninvited, as always, and I suddenly forget how to be human.

So I look down. Stare at the grass like it holds the answers the stars didn't.

I make it through, somehow. But the damage is done. I'm not really there anymore. Just a ghost trying to smile through dry lips and hide the tremor in my hands. Steven — nice guy, husband of Sheena's best friend — does his best to keep me looped in, but I'm barely hanging on. Every crackle of the fire, every flicker of that damn toy lightsaber from the kids, is pulling me under.

I can't say anything. How do you explain that a child's toy reminded you of a crash scene? That the lights brought the smell of diesel and death with them? You don't. You just nod, sip your drink, and pray for the night to end.

And when it does, I lie. I smile. I say "I had a great time" while my insides are screaming. Then I stay up all night on the balcony, watching the stars mock me again.

I cried. I don't say that for pity. I say it because it happened. Because I stood there, bone-tired and hollow, whispering for my mom like a goddamn six-year-old.

I've been told things get better. That therapy is a long road and ghosts eventually get tired of haunting you. I want to believe that. Really, I do. But most nights, I still end up alone under the vastness, begging the universe for a truce. Just a little peace. Just one night without the noise.

I'm not asking to be happy. I'd settle for still.

Until then, I keep showing up. Keep pretending. Keep writing.

And yeah... sometimes, I still wish upon a star.

# A Town Called Enough

There's a certain poetry in trading neon for starlight. You ditch the city — its clatter, its chaos, its car alarms and caffeinated ambition — and you end up somewhere like this. A small town. A quiet one. The kind of place where the air smells like earth instead of exhaust. Where your name means something, and your coffee comes with conversation, not a corporate logo.

Back in the city, everything's a sprint. You're always late for something: a meeting, a party, a deadline, a train. You chase moments like they're lottery tickets, hoping one pays off. But mostly, they don't. Mostly, they slip through your fingers while you tell yourself you're "living the dream." That is, until you realize it's someone else's dream and you're just the extra in the montage.

And then, like some cliché in a feel-good indie flick, you end up here — where time moves like molasses and people talk like they mean it. You hear birds instead of sirens. Wind through trees instead of wind through traffic. Your heart rate slows. Your shoulders drop. You start noticing things, like the way the morning light dances on a chipped fence, or how silence isn't silence at all — it's just a softer kind of sound.

Out here, solitude doesn't sting. It soothes. It whispers, *"Welcome back, stranger."*

The truth is, I didn't even know I was lost until I heard myself think again. Until I tasted stillness. Until someone said "good morning" and meant it. It's not glamorous. There's no velvet rope, no rooftop bars. Just porches and gravel roads and people who ask how you're doing — and wait for the answer.

I'm not saying the city's evil. Hell, I love the city. She's a gorgeous mess. She'll chew you up, kiss you slow, and ghost you before you've zipped your jacket. But out here? Out here is different. Out here doesn't want anything from you — just your presence. Out here, *you matter,* and not because of your resume or your wardrobe or who you know.

In a small town, value isn't assigned. It's recognized.

I found my footing in Falkland. That quiet little valley where the pines outnumber the people and the stars don't compete with street-lights. Where the biggest drama is whether the café ran out of pie. And somehow, that's enough. More than enough. It's grounding. Healing. The kind of place where you don't need to perform. You just need to show up.

And that's the thing — sometimes, just *being* is the whole damn miracle.

So yeah, maybe I'm not who I thought I'd be. I'm not some hotshot pacing an office with skyline views and a Scotch in hand. But I wake up, sip coffee with the sun, and know my neighbors' names. I sit on my porch and watch clouds drift like slow thoughts. And when I breathe, it doesn't feel like a task — it feels like *living.*

That's the trade-off. The rush for the real. The noise for the nuance.

In the city, you chase.
Here? You arrive.
Poetry indeed.

# Skates, Dreams, and Mustard Helmets

Last night, I watched a bunch of grown men chase a black rubber disc across frozen water while the whole damn country held its breath. A national ritual. A communion of hearts wrapped in red jerseys, each one screaming for glory, for gold, for a flicker of that childhood dream. We didn't win — but we lived. And in Canada, sometimes that's enough. Hell, anywhere, sometimes that's enough.

See, hockey isn't just a sport here. It's the heartbeat of the frozen north. The religion of backyard rinks and Saturday night sermons broadcast from living rooms and dive bars alike. It's the smell of sweat and sharpening steel. It's an 11-year-old with a crooked stick pretending to be Gretzky, Modano, Bure, Linden — a lineup of gods for those of us who prayed on ice instead of in pews.

Once, that 11-year-old was me.

I wasn't gliding across the surface like they do. I was stumbling through slush and hope on a frozen lake, narrating my own play-by-play because nobody else was watching. My crowd? The creak of winter trees and the whispering wind — nature's version of cheering. I'd shoot, I'd score, I'd raise my arms to the sky like I was holding the Cup instead of a tree branch. It felt real. Until it didn't.

Reality had cancer. She was five-foot-nothing and dying slowly in a hospital room overlooking McGuire Lake. On her good days, she let me dream out loud. On her bad days, we just sat in silence while I pretended not to be scared. I wanted to play hockey more than anything, but I knew we couldn't afford it — not with chemo bills and food banks being the financial plan.

And then, a miracle — not the kind wrapped in angel wings or dramatic lighting. Just a quiet kindness from someone in church. They paid for my registration. Gave my mom a little cash to get me gear. That's when she called from the Calgary cancer treatment centre to say she got me a helmet and skates. I cried when I hung up. I was going to be a hockey player.

The helmet was mustard yellow — not gold, not even Vegas gold, just French's yellow. The skates? Leather fossils with metal tubes — I'm pretty sure Moses used them to cross the Red Sea. But still, I had gear. I had ice time. I had a shot.

And yet... I almost didn't go. Thirteen is a brutal age to be different. Everyone else had shiny gear, team socks, parents who could afford tape that wasn't peeling off second-hand sticks. I had Depression-era gloves and enough self-doubt to fill a penalty box.

First practice. I show up looking like the thrift store version of a player. Everyone else looked like a future NHL highlight reel — I looked like a deleted scene from Slap Shot. I couldn't skate. Couldn't stop. Could barely stand. The other kids laughed. The parents laughed. All except one.

She left mid-practice. Came back later. Waited until we were done.

"Matthew?" she asked.

"Yes, ma'am."

"These should fit." She handed me a pair of used but beautiful skates. Modern. Functional. Laced with grace.

"Tyler outgrew them," she said. "They're yours now."

I told her I didn't have money. She told me not to worry about it. And in that moment, kindness skated in where confidence used to be.

I didn't become a star. Hell, I barely stayed upright. But I played. For a few seasons, I played. And once, I even got to share the ice with my best friend — Drew. He passed me the puck even though I missed more often than not. That's friendship. That's hockey. That's Drew.

So no, we didn't get the win last night. But we got the story. We got to watch kids-turned-men play the game they fell in love with in backyards, church leagues, and frozen lakes. We got poetry on ice. We got reminders.

Dreams don't always arrive shiny and new. Sometimes they show up chipped and bruised, wearing mustard helmets and smelling faintly of second-hand smoke. But they arrive.

So here's to the next face-off. To the kids chasing pucks and pipe dreams. To the ones who still believe in buzzer-beaters and magic on blades.

Here's to hockey — not just the game, but the grace that comes with it.

# Three A.M. and a Side of Cranberry Lies

It's three in the goddamn morning on Turkey Day and I'm wide awake. Not because of a nightmare or some PTSD-induced jump scare cooked up by my subconscious. No, this isn't that kind of story. I just... woke up. Sometimes the silence is so loud it taps you on the shoulder like an old friend you'd rather avoid but can't ignore. So here I am — upright, underwhelmed, and unburdened by sleep.

Normally, waking up this early would feel like a punishment from the gods of insomnia. But not today. Today is different. Today is Thanksgiving, and with the awareness of the date came a memory — one that refuses to tiptoe, barging in like a drunk uncle with a story no one asked for.

Flashback: Canadian Forces Base Borden, Ontario. 2004. The chow hall. Picture the world's saddest buffet. A plastic cup of possibly-milk, a tray featuring turkey so dry it moonlighted as sandpaper, vegetables that had the charisma of cardboard, and a scoop of mashed potatoes whose only seasoning was despair. Oh, and something that was supposedly cranberry sauce but looked more like it escaped from a failed science experiment.

That was dinner. A room with eighty empty tables and maybe four souls sitting as quietly as ghosts in a library. No chatter, no laughter, just fluorescent lights hissing like pissed-off snakes and the occasional scrape of a fork against a plate. Yet, for all its silence, it was one of the loudest rooms I've ever sat in.

I was alone. Not just alone in geography, but in spirit. My platoon had leave passes, places to go, families to return to. Me? I had radioactive cranberry sauce and a mother who, in her infinite grace, had dubbed me a "horrible, selfish little bastard." Why? Because I had joined the military and, in her mind, that meant I should now be financially capable of buying her a house. When I told her that wasn't exactly in the cards, she slammed the emotional door shut. For two years. Wouldn't take my calls. Pretended not to know who I was. Hallmark stuff.

Yeah, that Thanksgiving? It sucked. And yeah, I got invites from a few guys to tag along to their homes, but what's the point of pretending to be happy in someone else's picture-perfect living room when your own mother treats you like a stranger? I passed. Stayed behind. Ate my crime of a meal and stared at gravy like it held answers. It didn't.

Fast forward twenty years. I'm still up at three in the morning. Only now, it's not loneliness that wakes me. It's gratitude. It's anticipation. It's the absurd joy of knowing that I have a life worth waking up for.

These days, I live in British Columbia. The trees here are tall and whispery, like old souls who've seen some shit and fell gentle because of it. I've got a woman who once existed only in daydreams and heartbreak fantasies — Sheena — and two girls who let me call them "ours."

Two cats who think they own the place and two dogs who follow me like I'm a rock star on a farewell tour. It's chaos, but it's mine.

Tonight, I'll eat real turkey. With stuffing. And gravy that doesn't come out of a foil bag. I'll sit across from love instead of fluorescent bulbs. I'll laugh. Maybe cry a little — because, yeah, my mom's gone now. That's a wound that'll always twinge when the weather's just right. But I'm okay with that. We live long enough; we collect a few ghosts.

That night in Borden wasn't just sad. It was necessary. It gave contrast. A line in the sand so I could look back and say, "Christ, look how far we've come." I'm not that scrawny, wide-eyed kid anymore. Hell, I'm fat now. Soft around the edges. But for the first time, I know exactly where home is — not just a place, but a feeling. A family.

So today I'll cook. I'll snack. I'll yell at the TV during football. I'll put up Halloween decorations in the yard with frostbitten fingers and a full heart. I'll stand in the middle of this little town called Falkland and breathe deeply because for once, the air doesn't taste like solemnity.

Happy Thanksgiving, you beautiful bastards. Wherever you are, I hope you've found your home. And if you haven't yet, just keep going. It's out there — waiting for you, probably with burnt Brussels sprouts and questionable cranberry sauce. But believe me when I say this... it'll be the best thing you've ever tasted!

# Ghosts Don't Need Halloween

Halloween: a night for ghouls, goblins, and store-bought screams. People pay to be scared — they line up for haunted houses and chase that cheap high of synthetic terror. They want to be shaken. To flirt with fear in a way that's safe, that vanishes with the flip of a light switch.

But for some of us, fear isn't a thrill. It's not seasonal. It doesn't wear a rubber mask or hide behind plywood walls. No, real fear is personal. It has a key to your place and knows where you keep your memories. It waits for you, not in the dark, but in the mundane. In blood. In sound. In the way time folds in on itself when you're least ready for it.

I was reminded of this at the Haunting of Falkland: a small-town charity event designed to raise funds for first responders and community programs. I was volunteering with my buddy Kozy, playing monsters for the crowd. The kind of gig that lets you wear face paint and scare teenagers in a hallway. You know — fun.

The basement of the hall, where we were stationed, is rumored to be haunted. But I've seen ghosts. Real ones. And they don't knock.

Kozy cracked his head on a low-hanging vent during setup. One of those quick, stupid accidents that leaves you swearing and bleeding before you know what happened. I lit the wound with my flashlight. He was leaking. As heads tend to do. Nothing serious, but messy enough.

Upstairs, Kozy leaned over the sink. I went into autopilot. That old medic muscle memory kicked in; that peculiar calm that lives inside chaos. I was back in familiar territory, patching up a friend under too-bright lights, giving quiet instructions that feel like home.

And then it happened.

Kozy stood upright. He flicked his long hair back like a shampoo commercial gone wrong, and with it came a mist of water, sweat... and blood.

It hit my face before I could brace. Droplets. Red. Real.

And just like that, I wasn't there anymore.

I wasn't in Falkland. I wasn't at a Halloween fundraiser. I was somewhere else; kneeling on hot asphalt, holding someone's head together while time ran out. My body remembered everything before my mind had the chance to say, "Not now."

I froze. Heart racing. Breathing shallow. Blood on my skin, but not his blood. Still, it didn't matter. PTSD doesn't care about context. It doesn't care that you're okay. It just cracks the floor beneath you and drags you under.

And Kozy? He had no clue. He was washing his hands, probably thinking about duct tape or props or the next group coming through. That's the thing about ghosts; the ones we carry don't show up in photos. They don't leave footprints. They just live in your ribcage and strike when the moment's right.

Eventually, he noticed something was off. I must've gone pale or quiet or both. Without hesitation, Kozy shut down our section and walked me outside. No questions. No judgment. Just... care.

We stood along the fence in silence, the night wind slicing through the noise in my head. I apologized. Of course I did — because that's what you do when you break down in public, even when you shouldn't have to.

But Kozy didn't let me finish. He just shook his head and said, "There's nothing to be sorry for."

And that was it.

I didn't go back inside. Couldn't. I wasn't fit to scare anyone — not even myself. But I'll go back next weekend. Same event. Same basement. Different night.

Because that's what we do.

PTSD doesn't get the final word. It takes, sure. It rearranges you. But it doesn't get to keep you. Not unless you let it.

Me? I'm too damn stubborn. I breathe through it. I write through it. I walk into the fire knowing I've been burned before, but I'm still standing.

I know now that survival doesn't always look like a parade or a phoenix rising. Sometimes it's just a quiet breath in the dark. Sometimes it's saying, "I'll try again tomorrow."

Because the truth is: we don't choose our ghosts. But we do choose what we do when they show up.

And me?

I choose to wait for daylight.

# One Patch Left

The sky was that kind of perfect blue you only notice in hindsight — a soft, cinematic backdrop that didn't match the chaos clawing its way into history. September 11th, 2001. Just another Tuesday. Suits and coffees, cabs and crosswalks, the murmur of a city mid-sentence. Nobody knew the world was about to hemorrhage. Nobody knew the skyline was about to lose its breath.

I was eighteen. Just a kid with a crooked grin and the kind of invincibility only youth can afford. I watched it all from the safety of a television screen, the towers folding in on themselves like they'd had enough. News anchors choking on words that didn't exist yet. A whole world asking a question none of us could answer.

Four months later, I signed up. Canadian Armed Forces. Six and a half years of dust, sweat, and loss. My unit — 1 Field Ambulance — bled three names into foreign soil. Names I still carry in the corners of my mind like old Polaroids that won't fade.

Conspiracies? Politics? Miss me with all that. Today's not the day for tinfoil hats. Today's for remembering. For feeling. For bleeding a little with the people who still do, even after all these years. Because you don't need to be at Ground Zero to be touched by the fire.

Years after I traded camouflage for a paramedic uniform, I ended up drunk in the middle of Times Square. Lost in a crowd of millions, yet somehow invisible. That's the trick New York plays on you — it's a city that knows how to look right through you while somehow making you feel like you belong.

Across the street, I spotted an ambulance. Two medics inside trying to wrestle a few forkfuls of something vaguely resembling dinner before the city called them back. I had a patch in my pocket — my medic patch. It's tradition, among those of us in the trade, to hand one off to brothers and sisters in different cities. A little gesture that says, Hey, I see you. We're the same breed.

So I walked over. Introduced myself. Gave the patch.

The driver's name was George. Just George. No rank, no pretense. Turns out, George had been there. Not like me — watching from a living room in Canada. No. He'd been there. On the pile. In the smoke. Covered in someone else's dust, dragging bodies out of fire and heartbreak. A real one.

We talked for a bit — about the job, about the noise, about how no matter where you work, it always ends the same way: too many calls, not enough time, and something cold that used to be dinner. Then his radio went off, and George was gone, sirens chasing down another piece of somebody's worst day.

Before I left the city, I stopped at Ground Zero. Tried to make sense of it all. You can't. There's a weight there — not grief, not guilt. Something heavier. Something sacred. It presses into your bones and dares you to forget. You won't. You can't.

There's a bar nearby. The name's lost to whiskey and time. But inside, the walls are wallpapered with patches — police, fire, paramedics — stitched ghosts from all over the world. I had one patch left. I gave it to the bartender and pointed at the wall. Now it sits there, a tiny piece of Canada overlooking a room full of clinking glasses and half-healed wounds. Maybe someone notices it. Maybe they don't. Doesn't matter. It's there.

These days, I don't carry patches. Just stories. Scars. Empathy. That's what's left. That's what I give.

So New York — on this day, every year — you've got all of it. Whatever's left of my patched-up heart, it's yours. For George. For the ones who didn't walk out. For the ones who still can't sleep.

September 11th.

Never just a date. Always a scar that shaped the man. That shaped the world.

# Carnival Hearts and Cardiac Burgers

Life's a goddamn patchwork. A murky quilt of chaos and quiet stitched together by moments you didn't know were important until long after they'd passed. Most of it's noise — bills, obligations, that weird guy at the post office who talks too close. But every so often, there's a sliver of something worth holding onto. A flicker. A firefly in a jar. Something that reminds you you're still here. Still human. Still you.

Yesterday, in the molten hangover of a late summer sun that refused to check the calendar, I found myself at the Interior Provincial Exhibition in Armstrong. The IPE. For those not in the know, that's a fair — a real, old-school carnival — complete with screaming kids, overpriced lemonade, and the smell of deep-fried perfection mingled with livestock and hay bales.

Now, I know what you're thinking — Heneghan at a fair? Isn't that like sticking a Hemingway novel into a Teletubbies episode? And yeah, you'd be right. I don't do crowds. I don't do flashing lights. I definitely don't do Tilt-a-Whirls run by guys who look like they live in the back of a Pontiac Sunfire. No offence. But there I was. With my girls. With her. And that made all the difference.

PTSD, for the uninitiated, is like walking around with a live grenade in your chest. One wrong sound, one flash of light, one too-loud laugh at the wrong angle, and boom — you're not at the fair anymore. You're somewhere else. Somewhere loud. Somewhere hot. Somewhere you promised yourself you'd never go back to.

But yesterday? Yesterday, I didn't blow up. I just sweated through my shirt like a normal, emotionally constipated Canadian man in public.

We got through the gates, which are less gates and more cattle chutes designed to slowly extract your will to live. Once inside, the smells hit me like a two-step punch: cotton candy uppercut, manure jab. A hay-scented headlock brought it all together — a fragrance only a carnie could love. And you know what? It kind of worked.

The sounds were familiar, like an old mixtape you forgot you made: the hiss of hydraulics, the low hum of teenage rebellion, a random scream that almost sent me running for the exit. But I stayed. I stayed because it mattered. Because they mattered. And because I was starting to remember what magic used to feel like.

After a brief parental finance meeting where we dispensed with cash for the kids, we sat down. And then came the food.

Let me tell you about this burger. Holy hell. It was sin on a bun. A glorious, greasy confession of cheese, char, and caramelized onions. I bit into it like it had personally wronged me in another life. I moaned. Loudly. I think someone filmed it.

We people-watched like retired CIA operatives. Saw a couple break up. Tears and all. Watched a lady verbally eviscerate her boyfriend with the finesse of a Shakespearean villain. Guy looked like a hungover bobblehead. I almost offered him my onion rings as a peace treaty.

And as the day turned to dusk, and dusk into that glowing carnival night — where everything's tinted in neon and nostalgia — I started to drift. Not in the bad way. In the good way. I remembered my brother, Drew. Us as kids, wide-eyed and dumb, making memories we didn't know we'd need someday. And how he never once judged me for saying "nah, I'll sit this ride out." That kind of friendship is rare. Pure. Uncomplicated.

This was the first fair I've been to since PTSD tried to rent out space in my skull. Seven years of telling myself it wasn't possible. Seven years of believing the grenade was always live. And yet... there I was. Under flickering bulbs and the roar of carnival games, holding hands with a woman who once existed only in the soft-focus dreamscape of lonely nights. My Sheena. My anchor. My unwavering cheat code to surviving the storm.

Yesterday wasn't just a fair. It was a moment. My moment. A memory I get to keep. A little patch sewn into that crooked quilt of mine. Frayed at the edges, sure — but still holding.

That was my IPE.

How was yours?

# Where There's Smoke, There's Us

Life doesn't always knock. Sometimes it just kicks the door in and sets your world on fire — metaphorically, or, if you live in British Columbia, literally.

You go to bed thinking about leftovers and bills, maybe wondering why the hell your dog keeps licking the couch — and then boom, you wake up to an evacuation notice, a wall of smoke, and skies painted apocalyptic orange. Life, like fire, doesn't care about your plans. It just burns.

British Columbia — God's country, if God was into snow-caps, salty air, and charging you $18 for brunch. It's beautiful here. It's also brutal. We live among jagged postcard edges of mountain majesty that double as Mother Nature's tinderbox come August. We don't just exist here, we survive. And that survival turns into pride — the kind of pride that follows you when you leave, shows up in barstool stories about glacier lakes and hidden trails, the kind you only share with people who've earned it.

This place? It gets in your blood. Which is probably why we get so damn fired up when the fires do. We want answers. We want helicopters, retardant, reinforcements. We want someone to blame, because watching your home go up in smoke isn't something you can just "Namaste" your way through.

But here's the thing — while the rest of us are online demanding better strategy and stronger leadership, there are kids out there — kids — marching straight into the mouth of hell, gripping hoses like medieval swords. These men and women aren't Marvel characters. They don't have theme music or stunt doubles. They have ash in their lungs and twenty minutes of sleep under a pine tree that might not be there in the morning.

And still, they go.

Even when they're being cursed out in comment sections or shouted down in grocery stores. Even when someone's yelling that their cousin's cousin had to wet their roof with a garden hose alone. They keep going.

You want to know what real courage looks like? It's not in speeches. It's in soot-covered faces and cracked lips. It's in silence. In the way they show up, again and again, with zero applause and no guarantees. They don't do it for your thank-you(s), but maybe they should hear them anyway.

So this one's for the wildfire crews. For the dispatchers working 20-hour shifts with voices that never crack. For the pilots skimming treetops like daredevils in borrowed time. For the medics. The volunteers. The ones holding the line and the ones cleaning up after.

You are the reason we still have homes. Still have hope.

I've lost things to fire. Not as much as some. More than others. And yeah, I get mad too. But I also remember: fire is wild. And so is life. You don't always get control — just the chance to be human in the face of chaos.

So, if you're out there in the thick of it — sweating, aching, doubting if it matters — let me say this plainly: it does. You do. You matter. You're seen. You're needed. And if no one's told you lately, thank you. For the love of God, thank you.

Stay safe. And for those who've lost everything... you're not alone. This province may burn, but it also rebuilds. Together.

That's how we do it in Beautiful British Columbia — ash, scars, and all.

# Born Again Canadian

I wasn't born Canadian. I became Canadian.

It didn't involve maple syrup baptisms or pledging allegiance to Tim Hortons, though that wouldn't be a bad way to do it. I immigrated here when I was five. Still wobbly on my life legs, full of wonder, and not yet cynical enough to question why "toque" is spelled like a French insult but worn like a badge of honour.

For a kid, assimilation is less about borders and more about discovery. My first true taste of this new home? Root beer. Yeah. That syrupy brown mystery potion that tastes like minty molasses and freedom. Add a scoop of ice cream and suddenly I wasn't just in Canada—I was Canada. Wide-eyed. Sugar high. Politely burping apologies.

Fast-forward to 1994. I was handed a little paper certificate, sang a song about standing on guard, and officially became a Canadian citizen. That moment meant something. Still does. I didn't inherit this country — I earned it. I chose it. That's a different kind of love story.

Now, I promised no history lesson, but indulge me for a hot second. July 1st, 1867: three colonies joined forces under the British North

America Act and said, "Hey, we're tired of being everyone's polite younger sibling. Let's do our own thing." And they did. No guns. No guillotines. Just paperwork and passive-aggressive sovereignty. That's the Canadian way.

Since then, we've become a patchwork quilt of contradictions: we apologize like it's punctuation, but we'll throw down over a parking spot at Costco. We're the land of hockey fights and healthcare. We grumble about the cold, then cry when the snow melts. And that's what I love about us — we're complex, inconsistent, and relentlessly kind. We're the human version of a dog in a raincoat: unsure, a little awkward, but impossible not to love.

I got the privilege of serving this country in the Armed Forces for nearly seven years. Wore the uniform. Saluted the flag. Stood on guard for thee. Not for accolades. Not for medals. But because I believed in the idea of this place. A place that says, "You belong, eh?" no matter your past, passport, or accent.

And yeah, I wear plaid like it's Gucci. I eat poutine like it's soul food. I don't flinch when a moose crosses the highway or when someone says, "You good, bud?" with concern and condescension in equal measure. This is my home. My weird, cold, beautiful, bilingual home.

So this Canada Day, while the fireworks echo off the lake and the BBQ smoke rises like some kind of prairie incense, take a moment. Think about what it means to be Canadian. Not just the clichés — though, God bless every one of 'em — but the truth underneath: that we're a country built on difference, united by decency. And occasionally, duct tape.

We're not perfect. Never will be. But we try. And that's what makes this mess worth loving.

Happy Canada Day, you beautiful bastards. Let's raise a glass, pass the syrup, and keep this wonderous country going — one "sorry" at a time.

# Summer Starts Here, Kid

To the grads:

It's here. That sacred, chaotic, last-day-of-school energy. The final locker slams echo like a victory gong. Textbooks are tossed like confetti, halls flooded with one part nostalgia and three parts "Get me the hell out of here." June, baby. It smells like freedom, lilacs, fresh-cut grass, and just the right amount of teenage rebellion.

The academic hamster wheel finally screeches to a halt. The teachers retreat into silence, the students vanish like smoke, and somewhere a janitor hums a Sinatra tune because he knows—he's survived another year. The bell rings one last time, and it's not just a bell, it's a damn starting gun.

Summer.

Not a season. A religion.

It's bonfires crackling on the beach while someone strums three chords badly on a half-tuned guitar. It's kissing someone you might forget the name of but never the way they looked at you. It's sweaty palms, stolen beers, and broken curfews. It's those nights when the air hums with electricity and the stars wink like they know what you're about to do—and approve.

It's ice cream headaches and chlorine-soaked hair. It's bike rides that stretch into dusk and back again. It's pool parties, drive-ins, midnight skinny-dips, and the holy grail of all summer moments: the spontaneous road trip. No plan, no map, just you, a full tank, and the kind of music that makes you believe in second chances.

For those of you tossing your grad caps into the air, this summer is different. It's your last first summer. The final lap before life starts asking real questions. Rent, taxes, careers, heartbreak—the grown-up stuff. But not yet. Not today. Today, the only thing you need to worry about is which direction to chase the sun.

I'm 41, and high school still haunts my dreams like a B-side Oasis song—messy, bittersweet, and full of that reckless, invincible magic. I remember my first real summer of freedom: walking the Salmon Arm Wharf like it was my own private boardwalk, eating ice cream until my stomach protested, never gaining a pound, never knowing how good I had it. If I squint just right, I can still see the sun hitting the lake like a disco ball.

So here's the thing:

Summer isn't about what you do. It's about how you feel. It's a time when the rules blur, when gravity loosens, when you finally, mercifully, get to be. It's your permission slip to live without a five-year plan. Screw plans. Make memories.

To the Class of ***[insert year here]***—your diploma isn't an ending, it's a launchpad. And this summer? It's your first flight. So fly messy. Fall in love with someone who quotes bad poetry. Stay up too late. Say yes to things that terrify you. And write it all down, because trust me, one day you'll want to remember how it felt.

The real world will come. It always does. But for now, let it wait. Summer's here. The stage is set. The script is blank.

Go write the hell out of it.

# Where Dust Still Talks

There's a place in town where the ghosts wear spurs and the wind carries stories in the dust. A quiet arena, silent for most of the year, stoic and sun-stained like the cowboys that once rode through it. You could drive right past and never give it more than a glance. But that would be a mistake — a big one.

See, for 362 days a year, this place plays possum. It sleeps. But come late May, the Falkland Stampede doesn't just wake up — it rises. Like thunder on four legs and heartbeats syncopated with the hoofbeats of history.

You step inside those gates and suddenly you're not in 2025 anymore. Hell no. You're somewhere else. Somewhere where boots matter more than boardroom titles, where manners haven't gone extinct, and where people still wave to strangers without wondering what they want in return.

This isn't just some patched-together rodeo with city-slicker sponsorships and choreographed dirt. No, this is the rodeo. The rodeo.

Falkland's soul, stitched into denim and leather and the callused palms of people who've known real work, real grit, and real community. A place where belt buckles say more about a man than any resume ever could.

For three days, the town shape-shifts into something electric. Burgers sizzle, curly fries fly, and the scent of horses, hay, and hot dogs mixes into something damn near holy. Kids run wild, lovers walk slow, and folks from all over gather like church on a Sunday — if Sunday came with broncs, bulls, and Budweiser.

And then, just like that, the lights dim, the crowd thins, and the arena exhales. The dirt settles. The ghosts go back to sleep.

But here's the thing about the Falkland Stampede — it never really leaves. It lingers. In the boots caked with dust weeks later. In the fading tan lines. In the stories that'll be retold until the next May rolls around. It's not an event, it's a pulse. One that beats just beneath the surface until it's time to ride again.

So go ahead, forget the skyline cities and boardroom rodeos. If you want to feel something real, raw, and wonderfully out of time — come to Falkland. Close your eyes in those stands, listen close, and you just might hear the dust whisper,

"See you next year, cowboy."

# The Voice That Called the Game

There are voices, and then there are voices — the kind that rattle around in your skull long after the TV's gone black. Darren Dutchyshen was the latter. A voice like gravel wrapped in velvet, dipped in rye whiskey, and delivered with a wink. You didn't just hear Dutch — you felt him.

He wasn't just broadcasting sports. He was telling bedtime stories for grown men. Stats wrapped in soul. A highlight reel with a heartbeat.

I found out Dutch was gone while nursing a bitter cup of coffee — the kind that tastes like regret and keeps your hands warm enough to distract you from the chill that sneaks in when the world loses someone like him. There it was:

"Darren Dutchyshen, 1966–2024."

Like someone had yanked a page out of my youth and set it on fire.

I grew up with Dutch. Mornings before school, evenings when life felt like a mess and sports were the only thing that made sense. He had that rare gift — the ability to make you give a damn about curling, baseball, golf, cricket, maybe even synchronized swimming if he had enough time and a punchline for it. He was TSN's answer to your favorite uncle: sharp, hilarious, and always a little inappropriate in the best way.

He wore suits, but his vibe was all sweatpants and backyard beers. He talked to you, not at you — a subtle art most broadcaster's butcher. You got the sense he actually liked sports, which is surprisingly rare in that business. And when cancer tried to bench him, he got back in the game like the stubborn prairie storm he was — all wind and grit and laughter that wouldn't quit.

I never met the man. But I miss him like I did.

That's the thing about certain people — they sneak into your life through the screen and become part of your personal soundtrack. You don't remember the exact game he was calling or the punchline he delivered, but you remember how it made you feel. That's legacy. That's impact. That's Dutchy.

This isn't just a sports loss. This is our loss — for the misfits who found peace in a puck drop, for the kids who didn't have a dad but had Dutch at 5 PM sharp, and for anyone who ever needed a laugh served with a side of last night's scores.

So here's to you, Dutch.

For the mornings you made bearable,

For the nights you made better,

For the voice that called the game — and called it right.

Rest easy, big guy. The press box in the sky just got itself a ringer.

# Whiskey to Tea: A Love Letter to Mother's Day

There's a kind of Russian roulette to writing about Mother's Day. One chamber holds nostalgia. Another holds grief. A few are jammed with guilt, resentment, and the scent of perfume long gone stale. And if you're lucky, there's one loaded with love.

Today, I pulled the trigger.

Click.

Tea.

Not whiskey. Tea.

Not because I've turned into some kale-chewing zen-monk, but because something's changed. I have changed. And so has this day.

You see, Mother's Day used to hurt. Like clockwork, it rolled around with its pastel cards and brunch reservations and commercials full of perfect moms who look like they stepped out of a Disney+ original. I didn't have that. I had a woman who did her best... sometimes.

Other times, she did her worst. And I got both versions — the warm, smiling version who'd dance to old music in the kitchen, and the ghost with a scowl that could curdle milk. On some days, love. On others, porcelain angels turned projectiles.

But I'm not here to bury my mother. Not today.

I'm here to resurrect the day she left behind. And to tell you something strange and beautiful:

I've fallen in love with Mother's Day again.

Not because of the past, but because of the present — wrapped in the laughter of two mini-humans I didn't make but would die for. Because of a woman who builds furniture like a Viking and loves like a saint. Because of Sheena.

She's the real deal. Not perfect — God, no. She burns toast, loses her keys, cries during Subaru commercials. But she loves. Fully. Fiercely. Without agenda. I've watched her love those girls like the world might end tomorrow. And I've felt her love me — the broken, complicated, occasionally insufferable version of me. The only version.

She's taught me that motherhood isn't about Hallmark gloss. It's about sacrifice wrapped in laundry, about patience laced with caffeine, and about showing up. Every damn day. Even when it's hard. Especially when it's hard.

So now, when May rolls in and the tulips bloom, I don't look away. I look at her.

And I celebrate.

Not in spite of my mother, but because of her. Because somehow, from the wreckage of the past, I stumbled into a future worth writing about. A life with Sheena. A second chance at seeing what motherhood should look like.

So here's to you, mum. I'm not angry anymore. I'm grateful — for the good days, for the bad days, and for surviving them long enough to find someone who makes this day shine again.

And here's to Sheena — the woman who turned whiskey into tea and bitterness into awe.

Happy Mother's Day to all the warriors out there doing the world's toughest job without pay, without sleep, and without enough thanks.

You're the real magic in this madhouse.

# In Praise of the Women Who Save Us

There are certain truths in life you don't learn in school. No teacher pulls you aside in Grade 11 and tells you the world spins a little straighter because of women. No multiple-choice quiz teaches you that real strength isn't about shouting the loudest or lifting the heaviest — it's about showing up, day after day, for people who don't always deserve it. People like me.

I was raised by a single mother.

A complicated woman with a sharp tongue and a sharper wit. She laughed in the face of cancer — literally. When she lost her hair, she made jokes. When her breasts were taken from her, she shrugged and said, "Didn't need 'em anyway." That was her brand of strength. Raw. Sarcastic. Bulletproof. She wasn't a Hallmark card or a Lifetime movie. She was grit, personified. And I didn't know it then, but I was watching a masterclass in courage every day of my youth.

Later, I joined the military — because of course I did. Young men with something to prove often sign up to get yelled at and break themselves into something resembling useful. And there, among the shouting and sweating and testosterone, were women who outpaced me. Outran me. Outclassed me.

One of them — Allie — lapped me on a morning run. I was wheezing like a dying lawnmower, and she floated past like a goddess with a ponytail and combat boots. She didn't mock me. She encouraged me. She called back, "You've got this!" as if I wasn't busy dying. That moment stayed with me. Not because I caught up (I didn't), but because she extended grace where others might've dished out ridicule.

Grace. That's the throughline with all the incredible women I've known.

On the ambulance, I worked with countless female paramedics. Partners, not sidekicks. Brilliant, assertive, empathetic. Women who weren't afraid to call out bullshit — or bullshitters. Women who could cradle a dying child one call and then wrestle a drunk brawler to the ground the next. Women who never once asked to be compared to men — because they knew they were doing just fine without the metric.

And now... now I live with three women who humble me daily.

Sheena — my love, my saving grace, my daily dose of "how the hell did I get this lucky?" — is a mother, partner, warrior, and general contractor wrapped into one. She builds furniture, builds up children, builds up me. Her youngest daughter, diagnosed with Type 1 diabetes at five, takes life head-on. Gluten intolerance? Please. This kid's tougher than most grown men I know. Her oldest, thirteen and wise beyond her years, once stood beside me in a mall during Christmas — a place that might as well be Dante's eighth circle for a guy with PTSD.

I was spiraling. The crowds. The noise. The scent of overpriced perfume and capitalism. I felt my breath thinning. She saw it. This teenager. She didn't flinch. Just looked at me, said she wasn't going anywhere, and that we'd get through it together.

That's what women do. They stand with you. Even when they don't have to.

And look — I've done some hard things. I've zipped up body bags. I've broken terrible news to good people. I've knelt in blood and chaos and tried to will life back into broken bodies. But nothing — nothing — compares to the quiet, tireless strength I see in the women I live with.

My Sheena tends to my aching joints like a field medic and my fractured heart like a sculptor. She is the definition of grace under fire. And somehow, she still finds time to love me. A PTSD-riddled, emotionally dented man with more baggage than an airport carousel.

It's International Women's Day today.

And I'm sitting here feeling like the luckiest bastard alive.

To the women out there — the mothers, the daughters, the medics, the soldiers, the baristas who remember our names, the authors, the quiet warriors holding families together with duct tape and deadpan humour — thank you.

Thank you for teaching us that empathy isn't weakness.

That kindness isn't optional.

That love — real love — is a verb. A choice. A daily act of rebellion in a world that often forgets how.

And to the little girls growing up in this chaotic, beautiful mess we call life — may you never doubt your power. May you run faster than the boys, speak louder than the silence, and dare to take up space where none was offered.

In a world of Ewell's, be a Scout.

Hell, be you — bold, brilliant, and unrelenting.

Because the rest of us? We're just trying to keep up.

# The Year Santa Drove a GT Snow Racer

Christmas ends the way old lovers do — slow, quiet, and with more mess to clean up than you remember making. The garland starts to sag, the lights flicker with a little less purpose, and that charming tree in the corner morphs from yuletide symbol to living room hostage. It's like watching magic sober up.

But even as the season packs its bags, it leaves behind fingerprints. Ghosts of glimmer. Smells of cloves and pine that cling to your jacket. Memories that surface uninvited while you stir your coffee in a half-empty café, dodging clearance bins and the deflated joy of December's after-party.

That's where I was. Somewhere between a second-rate roast and a slow swirl of cream, watching the world come down from its seasonal high. The town still looked like Christmas had thrown up on it — half-price signs taped over full-price disappointment, and garlands that now resembled hangovers. Even the homeless guy on Fifth was in post-holiday form — same sign, different month. I gave him a burger once. He chucked it. Maybe he was keto.

I'd settled into my usual corner spot. The window was foggy, the coffee hot, and the view outside looked like someone had filmed a Tim Burton Christmas flick but forgot to add snow. A lone tree stood across the way — crooked, bare, and wind-whipped — a festive amputee with a single red bow flapping like a surrender flag.

Then the bell jingled. Father and son. The kid's voice was soft but audible:

"Wish we could go sledding... like last year."

That was the spark. One line. That's all it took. Suddenly I was ten again — Fly Hills, 1994. The air was sharper back then. So was life, oddly. The snow was thick, untouched, a perfect crime scene for reckless childhood joy. We rode plastic sleds like we were training for Olympic glory, carving up hills like sugar-high Vikings.

And then... it appeared. The Cadillac of sleds. The Mona Lisa of snow gear.

The Noma GT Snow Racer — Brett Hull Edition.

Royal blue. Pristine white. Yellow trim like it had been kissed by lightning. It even sounded fast. Our sleds, by comparison, were wet cardboard. We watched the thing descend the hill like a chariot sent from God — two kids and their dad riding glory straight into our fragile little egos. We didn't say a word. We just picked up our peasant toboggans and sulked home.

That year was thin. My mother was sick — a quiet kind of sick, the kind that doesn't ask for sympathy but bleeds it anyway. Money was tight. The house was quieter than usual. I didn't say much about the GT Snow Racer. Kids have this internal gauge for what not to say when a parent is treading water. And I already got the speech — "Christmas isn't about gifts."

Right.

Try explaining that to your ten-year-old self when Brett Hull's name is printed in bold on someone else's joyride.

Christmas morning came like a secret. The tree was modest. The sky, silver and still. I padded down the hallway, specs too big for my face and hope too small to expect much. But there they were — presents. Piles of them. Like someone had mistaken our house for a Hallmark movie. I tore into them, thrilled by action figures, toy weapons, and enough sugar to restart a heart. I was content.

And then...

"Might wanna get the door," my mother said.

There'd been no knock. Just her voice, smoke-wrapped and sleepy, holding the kind of mischief that only mothers and magicians know.

I opened the door to find one more box. Heavy. Decorated like it had been wrapped by elves on commission. I dragged it inside like it was a treasure chest from some long-lost Christmas shipwreck.

And there it was.

The logo. The colors. The name.

*NOMA GT SNOW RACER* — with Brett Hull Poster Inside.

Time stopped. My ten-year-old brain broke a little. I remember steam fogging up my glasses, my breath catching in my throat, and then that feeling... that pure, atomic joy that only Christmas can pull off. The kind that bypasses your brain and punches you right in the soul.

I turned to my mother, stammering like I'd just seen God in snow gear.

"...The one you wanted," she said.

Yeah. It was.

Years later, sitting alone in that café, watching trees forget how to be trees and listening to a kid pine for last year's snow, I realized something: Christmas doesn't end. It just waits. It tucks itself into the pockets of your coat, into memories that smell like pine and Marlboros. Into the spaces between grief and gratitude.

My mother's gone now. But that memory? That morning? That look on her face when I realized what she'd done — that lives forever.

Turns out Santa drives a GT Snow Racer. And sometimes... she smokes menthols.

Merry Christmas, folks.

Hold tight to the moments. They're the only gifts that don't need receipts.

# The War After the War

There's something about November that doesn't even try. The sky slouches over the earth in this dull, defeated grey — like it just woke up and realized hope packed up and left in the middle of the night. It's the kind of sky that doesn't offer a sunrise, just a slightly lighter shade of Rhino. Fitting, really. Because if grief had a forecast, it would look a hell of a lot like Remembrance Day.

We stand there, the lot of us, scattered like punctuation marks on a page that never ends. No words spoken. No need. Just the hush of winter's breath weaving between jackets and poppies. We gather to remember the young who never got the chance to grow old and the old who were once young enough to believe they'd live forever. We stand for the ones who gave everything — including the parts of themselves they never got back.

When I was young, war was just something that played between commercials. An abstraction. A headline. Another name carved into the screen while you shoveled cereal into your mouth and complained about math homework. But then I put on the uniform, and war stopped being a story — it became the reason behind everything I did. Every step I marched. Every drill I perfected. Every breath was laced with the quiet, omnipresent truth that this was all preparation for something I might not come home from.

The instructors we had weren't caricatures out of a boot camp movie. They were the real thing — just back from places the world tries to forget. Places with names that sound like tongue ties. They didn't tell stories so much as they let them bleed through the cracks in their armor — through silence, through thousand-yard stares, through the way their hands trembled when they didn't think anyone was looking.

During my time, I lost three brothers. Not metaphorically. Literally. I carried them. Escorted them. Watched them get lowered into the earth like secrets we didn't want to keep. Each casket swallowed by the soil left behind this impossible hole — not just in the ground, but in me. And in the years that followed, the phone kept ringing. More names. More losses. Not from gunfire or shrapnel, but from the aftershocks. From the quiet wars that rage when the shooting stops. Because not every battlefield has a zip code — some of them live behind your eyes.

At forty, I stand with lines on my face and ghosts in my chest. I stand in silence with the rest of them, and I feel every beat of my heart like it's dragging itself through thorns. That's the irony — we leave behind flowers, poppies, symbols of remembrance. But what we really leave behind is innocence. Naivety. The idea that we'll come home the same way we left. That illusion doesn't survive a tour.

There's a line you hear often around this time: "They shall not grow old, as we that are left grow old..." It used to sound poetic to me. Now it just sounds like truth carved in marble. Because I am growing old. I've earned every grey hair, every wrinkle, every scar. But those I lost?

They're frozen in time. Forever young. Forever perfect. And I carry their names like medals no one pinned on my chest.

Wilmot. Starker. Boomer. Penny. Rondeau. Atkin. Turner. Not just names — men. Women. Brothers. Sisters. Pieces of my past that refuse to stay there. They visit often, usually uninvited, usually late at night. I remember them. I always will. And not just on November 11th, though this is the day that stings the most.

It was supposed to be the war to end all wars. That's what they told us. But humanity's arrogance is undefeated. So we keep showing up, year after year, to honour the fallen and brace for whoever's next.

There's nothing glamorous about any of this. No Hollywood fade-outs or speeches that tie everything up with a bow. There's just the weight. The silence. And the memory of the man or woman who once stood in your place — now just a name, a face, a flag folded three times too tight.

So yeah, I remember. I remember the sound of boots on gravel. The laughter before a training exercise. The long drives in rattling silence. I remember the last phone calls and the hollow ring of "I'm sorry" from someone who informed us of the deaths.

Hush now. The guns are silent.

Rest easy, brothers and sisters.

We'll carry the rest.

Forever. Always. And longer.

# The Last Drink I Never Had

There was a time in my life — not too long ago — when I wasn't going to grow old. Not because of some romantic rebel streak or reckless rock-and-roll lifestyle. No, mine was slower. Quieter. The kind of suicide that happens in instalments. Pour by pour. Sip by sip. A long goodbye disguised as "just one more."

I wasn't drinking to have fun. I wasn't drinking to forget. I was drinking to not feel. There's a difference. Big one. And unless you've walked through the fire in combat boots or sat still while the world around you burned — you might not get it. And that's okay. I hope you never do.

I was a soldier once. That sentence alone should come with a warning label. I buried more brothers than birthdays. And when I left the service, I didn't. Not really. I simply changed uniforms and became a paramedic. Different job, same soundtrack. Sirens, blood, guilt. Sometimes, I think grief has a smell. For me, it was always antiseptic, diesel, and the faint scent of whisky on my breath.

They tell you that alcohol is a depressant. What they don't tell you is that it can also be a lullaby. A way to tuck in the chaos and rock it to sleep. For me, it was a cure for the noise. But cures have side effects. And booze? She always overcharges.

One night, some years ago, I took a walk. Not the kind your Apple Watch congratulates you for — the other kind. The kind of walk where the destination is silence. I ended up at the edge of the city on an overpass, a flask of Macallan 18 clutched in my hand like a crucifix. Fancy scotch for a final act. Classy, right? Maybe I just didn't want to die with cheap liquor on my breath. Maybe I thought if I was going out, I should do it like a man who still had taste.

The ghosts were loud that night. Every friend I'd lost, every life I couldn't save, every moment I chose a bottle over a conversation — they showed up for the occasion. The Devil doesn't wear horns. He whispers with your own voice. And he speaks in the language you understand best. Mine was always aged oak and amber promises.

What stopped me? That's a longer story. Maybe I'll tell it someday. What didn't stop me was logic. Or faith. Or hope. What stopped me was something else entirely. And the realization that there are choices you can't undo. Stepping off that ledge? That's one. But every drink before it? That's a decision you keep making. Until you don't.

August 12th, 2018. The day I told the Devil to piss off and poured the rest of that bottle down the drain instead of my throat. The day I started measuring my life in sunrises instead of shots.

It hasn't all been heroic and cinematic since then. There have been days when sobriety felt like a cruel joke. When grief came knocking again — hard. Like in 2020, when my sister died. The bottle started singing again, low and sweet. But a friend, Eric, showed up in the middle of all that noise. Stood tall between me and the siren song. No cape. No lecture. Just presence. Sometimes, that's all it takes. Someone standing still when you can't.

Now, five years later, I wake up without hangovers. Without regret leaking out of my pores. I've got a wife who somehow loves me anyway. Two kids who didn't sign up for a broken-down ex-medic with ghosts in his closet but show up every day with nothing but heart. I've got a circle of friends who've seen me at my worst and stayed anyway. That's not luck. That's grace.

So yeah — today's my soberversary. Big whoop, right? But it matters. Not because I've become some walking self-help manual, but because I didn't die. I stayed. I chose to stay. Over and over again.

My name is Matthew. I'm an alcoholic. But right now, in this moment, I'm just a man with a past, a second chance, and a damn good cup of coffee in his hand.

And no scotch.

Not today.

Not anymore.

# Don't Forget to Pack Hope

Here's life's dirty little secret: the longer you hang around, the more ghosts you collect. Doesn't matter how charming you are, how many sit-ups you do, or how many gluten-free power bowls you eat — death comes for all of us, and on the way to your own grave, you'll stop by a few others.

It starts small. A hamster. A grandma. Maybe some poor fish you overfed as a kid because you thought love was the answer to everything.

Then it gets personal.

Me? Death didn't just swing by for coffee. It moved in, slept on the couch, and left cigarette burns in all my memories.

When I was ten, my mother sat me down and casually told me she didn't feel like fighting her cancer. No grand metaphors. No teary-eyed hugs. Just a tap on the ass and "go play."

I didn't.

I cried.

She told me to stop.

I couldn't.

So she hit me.

And just like that, I learned to cry with the lights off.

Fast forward a couple decades and cancer had nothing on depression. She beat the big C, but not the monsters that whispered in her ear every night. In 2017, she killed herself. I got the news in the form of a phone call that lasted just under four minutes. That's all it took to demolish my reality while strangers outside my window laughed over lattes and honked in traffic like nothing happened.

Her suicide note? Three pages of soul-bleeding prose. I'd read a lot of those as a paramedic. Too many. But hers was the one that broke me. It started cold: "To my kids..." but dissolved into a haunting map of her undoing — heartbreak, rage, loneliness, and finally, resignation.

That same night, I had an anxiety attack that landed me in the ER. My buddy Eric — another broken soul in uniform — dragged me in.

"He's a vet," he told the triage nurse. "PTSD. Paramedic. His mom just died."

I heard it like it was about someone else. Someone pathetic. I didn't feel like a veteran. Or a man. Or anything remotely close to a person worth saving. I felt like a drunk. And an orphan. A cliché in a crumpled uniform.

My dad? Arrested when I was eight. Child abuse. Yeah, the hits kept coming.

So there I was, broken and splintered, with more baggage than an airport carousel. And finally, after a thousand drinks and even more bad decisions, I realized I was next in line for the grave. Death was holding the door open, and I was one scotch away from stepping through.

In 2018, I checked into rehab.

Rehab.

What a word. Sounds like a Silicon Valley startup, not a place where souls go to puke, shake, and unravel. But there I was. Sweating out years of poison in a sterile hallway full of ghosts who looked just like me.

There was no epiphany. No choir of angels. Just a blunt therapist with kind eyes and a voice like a scalpel.

"You're at a precipice," she said. "And you're running out of time."

That night, I packed. A toothbrush. A hoodie. My guilt. My shame. And one more thing.

A note I scribbled on a Post-it:

"Don't forget to pack hope."

That one stuck.

Detox was hell. My body turned on me like a jealous ex. The shakes. The sweats. The nightmares came back like bad sequels. I hadn't dreamt in years. I passed out instead of sleeping — booze will do that. Numbs you out. Kills the reels.

Then one day, the front desk paged me.

Mail.

From Heather. A publisher. The kind who still uses stamps. She sent a letter with instructions:

"Write it all down — the dark, the light, the bullshit in between. Write it down and keep going."

She believed in me. Said I was a writer. Said I had a story to tell.

She started sending little packages. Notes. Puzzles. A letter a day — literal letters. An anagram to piece together.

And in the quietest corners of a rehab library, under the golden glow of maybe the first kind light I'd known in years, I solved it:

*ONE DAY YOU WILL BE AN AWARD-WINNING AUTHOR.*

And I laughed. And I cried. And I wanted to believe her.

Cut to 2024. Shuswap Writers' Festival. Big competition. Real authors. Real pressure.

And guess what?

I won.

First place. Nonfiction.

The kid who used to pass out just to avoid dreaming? The guy who packed "hope" like it was contraband in a carry-on?

Yeah. That guy won.

And I wish I could tell you that was the end of the pain — but 2020 came. And so did the loss of my sister, Lisa. Another suicide. Another bottle trying to call my name. But Eric, that beautiful bastard, pulled me back again.

I still think about them — my mom and Lisa — every damn day. But now I do it sober. With a full heart. And yeah, with a few awards on my shelf and a pen in my hand.

So if you're out there — if your life feels like it's folding in on itself and you've got one eye on the exit — listen to me. Not as a hero. Or a writer. Or a man with the answers.

But as a guy who forgot how to cry and then remembered just in time.

**Don't forget to pack hope.**

You never know when you'll need it. Or how far it might take you.

# The Ring on My Ass

There's a faint circle on the back pocket of my jeans. A ghostly stamp. Faint. Smudged. Like the kiss of a memory that doesn't quite want to let go. I noticed it the other night after coming home from Olivia's hockey game — tired, satisfied, reeking faintly of rink fries and whatever tragic cologne lives inside a rec centre locker room.

At first, it puzzled me. I thought maybe I'd sat in something—chewing gum, spilled soda, the shattered ego of a dad whose kid missed a breakaway. But no. It came to me in a quiet, cinematic gasp. That ring? That worn-in halo? It's from my wallet. And inside that wallet lives a coin. A small, round, deceptively heavy reminder of everything I've been through. Of what I used to be. And who I damn well refuse to be again.

So let's start here: My name's Matthew, and I'm an alcoholic.

No applause, please. This isn't one of those Lifetime moments where a string swell kicks in and we all learn a lesson. I'm not interested in redemption porn. I'm just a guy who spent over a decade hiding from himself in a bottle, pouring grief into whiskey glasses and pretending the burn meant I still felt something.

I used to wear uniforms — soldier, medic, maybe even martyr if you squinted hard enough. What those uniforms left me with were memories soaked in blood, sweat, and the ghosts of brothers who never made it home. I carried their names like rosary beads, each one a prayer I wasn't brave enough to say out loud. I saved lives for a living while quietly dying on the inside. That's the gig. You're the calm in someone else's storm, while your own hurricane swirls just beneath your ribs.

And booze? That was the escape hatch I crawled through nightly. Until I couldn't crawl anymore. Until I stood at the edge — not metaphorically, not poetically, but really — and realized I had to choose: leap toward something terrifying and new... or stay still and rot. Spoiler alert: you're reading this. So I leapt.

In 2018, I walked into a trauma and addiction rehab facility and threw down my last drink. Six years later, I haven't picked one up since. And in my wallet — right where my ass cheeks are apparently now branded — lives the five-year sobriety coin my wife Sheena gave me last summer. It's not flashy. But it's mine. Proof that I didn't die when I could have. That I crawled out of the fire with burns, sure, but also with a heartbeat.

That circle on my jeans? That faint, dirty imprint? It's a goddamn badge of honor. And it showed up after a long, beautiful day watching a nine-year-old girl fly across a sheet of ice like it was her personal kingdom. Olivia skated, she shot, she scored. Then she searched the stands to make sure I saw her do it. And I did. Through clear eyes. Through sober eyes. Through eyes that have seen far too much darkness and still chose to stay open.

My name is Matthew, and I'm an alcoholic. That will never change. But here's what has: I don't hate myself anymore. I don't wake up wondering if I'll make it through the day. I don't drink. I feel. I cry. I love. And holy hell, do I feel grateful.

So yeah, there's a little ring on my back pocket. If you see it, give me a high-five. Maybe even slap my ass, if you're bold and consensual. Because that ring? That's not shame. That's survival. That's joy. That's me.

And this version of me? I kinda like him.

I said kind of!

# A Kid's Game and Other Lies We Tell Ourselves

They say baseball's just a game — a kid's game — played by grown-ass men in tight pants and million-dollar contracts. But they're wrong. Or at least, they're missing the point entirely. Because baseball is the closest thing we've got to time travel. One crack of the bat and you're back in a summer that never really happened the way you remember it. But it doesn't matter. Memory has always been more poet than historian.

It's a simple game, they say. Nine guys, a stick, a ball, and a dream. But beneath the surface — beneath the green cathedrals and overpriced beer — lives something bigger. Something that doesn't show up in box scores. Something that smells like cut grass, roasted peanuts, and the fleeting hope that the world outside those stadium walls might just wait for us to finish nine perfect innings.

I was never gonna make it to the big leagues. Hell, I wasn't even a Little League legend. I was the kid who struck out looking and then apologized to the ump for wasting his time. But I watched. I watched with the kind of devotion usually reserved for gods and crushes. The thwap of a fastball, the poetry of a well-turned double play, the gladiatorial standoff between pitcher and batter — all of it was church to me. Holy, messy, timeless.

And the crowd — man, the crowd. That's where the magic really happened. Not just in the seats, but in the space between people. The shared nachos. The matching jerseys. The fathers pointing out stats to bored sons. The mothers clutching toddlers with one hand and a beer with the other like they've done this dance a thousand times. That was the dream. The family that looked like a Norman Rockwell painting, even if it only lasted for nine innings.

I didn't have that growing up. My family life was more "Game of Thrones" than "Field of Dreams." No road trips to Fenway, no late nights under the lights. I grew up in a small town where dreams came to die quietly. But years later — as a broken-down ex-soldier, ex-medic, ex-everything — I found myself sitting in Yankee Stadium, shoulder to shoulder with my best friend, watching the Yankees and Mariners go to war under a New York sky.

And for a few hours... I was that kid again. The one who believed in the power of a well-hit ball and a bottom-of-the-ninth miracle. The one who thought maybe — just maybe — the world wasn't such a terrible place after all.

We ate street meat and laughed at knockoff merch vendors who swore their misspelled "Jeter" jerseys were "authentic." We watched the lights come on and the crowd rise for a home run that sent the Bronx into ecstasy. And I felt normal. Not healed, not whole, but normal. And when you've lived inside the wreckage of PTSD and grief for as long as I have, "normal" is a miracle.

That's the thing about baseball. It doesn't fix you. It just holds you for a little while. Gives you a place to be still. To remember who you were before the world got its claws in you.

So yeah, it's a kid's game. And that's exactly why I love it. Because somewhere under all this scar tissue and cynicism, that kid is still alive. Still watching. Still hoping.

And he's ready to play ball.

# Cupid, Whiskey, and the One That Stayed

Valentine's Day. A day for overpriced roses, shitty chocolate, and forced declarations of love in candlelit restaurants full of couples pretending not to regret their dinner reservations. Some call it beautiful. Others call it bullshit. I've called it both — sometimes on the same day.

Let's rewind to 2018 — the year Cupid took a dump in my whiskey glass. My mother was dead. I was single. The kind of single that makes loneliness feel like a goddamn sport. So I did what any emotionally constipated, grief-stricken drunk would do: I crawled into the darkest bar I could find and tried to pickle myself in single malt Scotch. Macallan 18, if you're wondering. Because even when you hate yourself, you still have standards.

That night, I wasn't drinking to feel good. I was drinking to disappear. The kind of drunk where your body stays behind, but your soul slips out the back door. Eventually, I got cut off — a bartender's polite way of saying, "You've reached the point where even capitalism can't justify serving you." So I stumbled out into the cold, wandering the city like a ghost in boots. Eye contact became a challenge to strangers. A drunken dare. No one took the bait. Just one guy lost in a blur of neon and heart-shaped bullshit.

I ended up on a bench downtown, surrounded by flickering signs, flower-toting lovers, and the hollow hum of modern romance. I was breathing, but not really alive. Just waiting for the snow to bury me.

Fast forward one year. Valentine's Day 2019. I was sober now. Suit and tie. Standing backstage at a storytelling event. This time, the glass was empty — and so was the hole where booze used to live. In its place? Something else. Still hollow, but less jagged. I was about to go on stage and talk about my mom. Her cooking. Her suicide. Yeah, it's a hell of a jump in tone — welcome to my life.

Halfway through my story, I cracked. Broke down. Couldn't talk. Couldn't breathe. A gasp from the audience pulled me back. I wiped my face, pulled it together, and finished the tale. When I did, people stood. They clapped like I'd just cured cancer. I think they were just glad I survived the retelling.

Then came the old man. Hunched, slow-moving, arthritic as hell. He put a hand on my shoulder and told me my story brought back the smell of his mother's apple pie — the kind of memory you don't expect to find in a community centre on Valentine's Day. He called my writing a gift. Said I should keep doing it. So I did. Still am.

And then came her.

February 2021. Same date. Different city. Different man. I was on a couch next to the woman I love. The kind of woman who lights candles without trying. Who makes you forget that you ever hated February in the first place. We made a pact not to do gifts. Naturally, we both broke it. Of course we did. That's love — saying one thing and meaning another, wrapped in gift paper and cheap bows.

We exchanged trinkets. Smiled. Cuddled under a blanket. I leaned in for a kiss, and... yeah. That's when it happened. The fart heard 'round the world. A seismic shift in romance. The cats ran. She laughed so hard I thought she might pass out. Me? I turned crimson and laughed with her. Because that's what you do when love shows up in the form of bodily betrayal. You embrace it. You kiss anyway. And you realize... damn, I might just be happy.

So yeah, Valentine's Day. Once a punchline, now a plot twist. A reminder that sometimes the worst days can become something else entirely — a stage, a story, a fart on the couch next to the love of your life.

If today sucks, hang tight. Cupid's got bad aim, but eventually he hits something worth holding onto.

Happy Valentine's Day, you beautiful bastards.

# The Honk Heard 'Round the Block

I live in a small town — the kind of town that doesn't show up on Google Maps unless you already know it's there. It's not famous. It's not Instagrammable. And that's precisely the point. It's guarded by trees the size of teenage dreams and hugged by mountains that seem like they're trying to hold the sky together.

People either call this place home or a place they stopped for gas and a bathroom break. But if you stick around long enough, maybe drink the coffee, breathe the air, walk barefoot in the summer grass — this little dot on the map has a way of wrapping itself around your ribcage and never letting go.

Three years ago, I stumbled into it — heart ragged, soul a bit threadbare — and under a galaxy of stars so arrogant they didn't even bother blinking, I fell in love. With the sky. With the silence. With the stillness that didn't ask me to perform or pretend. It was the first place I'd been where the world didn't whisper, "You're behind."

Summers here are green enough to make poets jealous. The fall? Think golden leaves doing a slow striptease for the wind. And there's this golf course — more myth than manicured — hidden away like a local secret too good for tourists.

But that's not what I came to tell you.

This story is about a honk.

Not the kind that wakes you up at 2 a.m. in a city that forgot how to be quiet. No, this was a different kind of honk — the kind that made my wife and I stop mid-dishes one night and ask, "What the hell is that?"

Every evening, like clockwork, this colossal rig would lurch up the incline outside our house and give a honk. Just once. Maybe twice. Like a friendly ghost who used diesel. Naturally, we did what any curious humans would do — we theorized.

"Sheena," I said, "maybe he's warning deer."

"Or kids," she said. "Maybe he's a really polite menace."

"Or maybe," I said, "he just likes to hear himself honk."

But then one evening, elbow-deep in a pan that wouldn't come clean, I glanced out the window and saw it. The truck. The driver. Big rig. Bigger heart. He was idling in front of a house — not ours — and waving.

That's it. Just a wave.

A few days later, we passed that same house on our way out of town and there it was: a little boy, perched on the back of his couch, face smooshed to the window, waving like his arm owed the world money.

That's when it clicked. The honk wasn't random. It wasn't a warning or some small-town Morse code. It was a daily love letter to a boy in a window.

So the next night, I stood watch.

Nothing.

No honk. No headlights. Just my own breath fogging up the glass and the quiet drip of a kettle whistling its loneliness.

Then, just as I surrendered to disappointment, it came:

HOOONK. HOOOOONK.

I dashed to the window like a kid on Christmas and saw the truck, waving driver, and that same kid — grinning like joy itself was contagious. And as if the scene needed a cherry on top, out popped a dog from the cab. A mutt. A scruffy, stubby-legged co-pilot in a high-vis vest. Of course he had a vest. Every working-class hero has a sidekick.

I stood there, smirking like a fool. Because somehow, in a world gone cynical, this moment existed. A kid. A truck. A dog in a vest. And me — a grown man rediscovering wonder while holding a mug of tea.

We don't get many miracles. But we get honks. And sometimes that's enough.

So yeah, I live in a small town. Maybe you've never heard of it. Maybe that's the magic. Maybe it's the kind of place that lets you slow down just enough to notice the poetry in the mundane. A place where love looks like steel and rubber and sounds like a horn on a quiet night.

Come visit sometime. Roll your windows down. And for the kid in the window — give a little honk.

He's listening.

So am I.

# Dirty Thirty's Final Act (or: How Not to Die Stupid at 40)

So here we are. The last lap of my thirties. It's not so much a birthday as it is a border crossing. No confetti, no marching band — just a guy holding a wrinkled passport and a look that says, "Did I actually survive all that?" Somehow, yeah.

Before I officially join the Forty Club — population: stiff joints and unsolicited advice — I figured I'd drop a few crumbs of wisdom I've picked up along the way. Take 'em or leave 'em. But they've kept me breathing, mostly upright, and occasionally even happy.

1. Say "I love you." Often.

Don't be stingy with your I-love-you(s). The world's already hoarding enough silence. And when someone you care about slips away — which they will — you'll never regret saying too much. Only too little. So say the thing. Mean it. And say it again.

2. Be as kind to yourself as you are to strangers.

This one? Still working on it. The guy in my mirror is a real prick some mornings. But I try. And when I fail, I try again. That's the gig. You wouldn't kick a friend while they're down. So why do it to yourself?

3. Being late isn't a war crime.

I used to think tardiness was akin to treason. Military habits die hard. But these days? If I'm late picking up the kid, I don't spiral. I breathe. I apologize. I move on. Most people won't remember your lateness. They'll remember how you made them feel when you showed up.

4. Someone else's cruelty isn't your autobiography.

Some folks will try to dim your light just because theirs flickered out. Let them. You're not required to carry their baggage just because they dumped it at your feet. Nod. Walk on.

5. Failure is a comma, not a full stop.

You're going to fall flat. You're going to look stupid. And it's going to suck. But guess what? That's the toll booth to greatness. Pay up, learn something, and keep going.

6. Be humble.

Humility isn't about thinking less of yourself — it's about thinking about yourself...less. Arrogance builds walls. Humility opens doors. Walk through the right one.

7. Love is not a Netflix special.

There's no dramatic kiss in the rain, no sweeping orchestral score. There's just two flawed humans choosing each other over and over again. Through burnt toast, bad moods, and fart-filled cuddles. Love isn't effortless. It's effort — and that's what makes it real.

8. It's okay to be a mess sometimes.

Life's not a polished Instagram reel. It's spilled coffee, unwashed hair, and wondering if your dog judges your playlist. Let yourself fall apart. Just remember to get back up.

9. Tomorrow is a maybe.

Don't save your best shirt for "someday." Don't wait to be happy. Don't put off joy like it's a dentist appointment. Be here. Now. The present is the only currency that never devalues.

10. Time's not a number. It's a fuse.

We're all ticking. That's not morbid. That's motivation. Don't waste your minutes pretending you're immortal. Wake up, whisper something you're grateful for, and then go raise a little hell — or at least make someone smile.

And that's it. My unsolicited wisdom before I cross the 40-yard line. No balloons. No gold watches. Just a grateful heart, a few scars, and the stubborn belief that the best parts might still be ahead.

So thanks for reading. Thanks for being here. Thanks for loving me — even when I've been a self-loathing mess with a half-eaten sandwich and three-day-old thoughts.

Here's to 40.

Let's make it weird.

# Ghosts of Christmas Me

It starts, as most sad stories do, with a boy.

Not the kind of boy who breaks windows or rides bikes downhill with reckless abandon. No, this kid was the wallpaper. Quiet. Out of the way. The kind of kid who learned early how to fold into the background so no one would notice he didn't quite belong. He was soft-spoken, unsure, and always a little off-beat — like jazz without the cool.

He wasn't looking for much. Just a little warmth. A little love. Maybe a hand on the shoulder that didn't come with conditions or consequence. But mostly, he got silence. The kind that hums loud enough to make you believe it's your fault.

Time, that indifferent bastard, rolled on. The boy got older. Christmases came and went — some with cheap tinsel, most with cheaper memories. Eventually, that boy became a man, the kind with a heavy head and heavier heart. Still quiet. Still searching.

Cut to a Christmas Eve — one of many — where this not-quite-boy, not-quite-man found himself seated in the loneliest place on Earth: a half-empty movie theatre showing something utterly forgettable. He wasn't there for the film. He was there because it was open. Because it asked nothing of him. Because it was warm, and he wasn't.

Popcorn. Twizzlers. Medium Coke. Christmas dinner for one. A sad little ritual dressed up as tradition. Halfway through the movie, like clockwork, he'd unzip his jacket, fish out his flask, and baptize that Coke with something stronger. Scotch, usually. The good stuff, if you can believe it. A little sip of oblivion dressed in Christmas lights.

Then the credits would roll, and the house lights would burn a little too bright for a man that hollow. He'd trudge through snow and broken streetlights, past men sleeping in bus shelters and cardboard cathedrals. He'd wonder how they got there — and if he was really any different.

Most nights, he'd end up in this grim little bar wedged between a pawn shop and a bail bondsman. The kind of place where souls went to expire slowly over a well drink. The lights were too bright, the music too sad, the bartender too quiet. It was perfect.

He'd drink. He'd sulk. He'd talk to ghosts — a little girl he couldn't save, a burned man he couldn't forget. Paramedic ghosts, paramedic guilt, clinking glasses with memories that wouldn't stay dead. If Dickens wrote Pulp Fiction, this would be the Christmas special.

"So... this is Christmas?" he'd think.

Yeah, kid. This was Christmas. Back then.

But here's the kicker — time didn't stop. It didn't freeze him in place. Somehow, the boy crawled out of the theater, out of the bar, out of the wreckage. Slowly. Quietly. Desperately. And now, he's forty. He's older, wiser, still a little haunted — but he's loved. He's not sipping sadness from a paper cup in the dark anymore. He's got a home. A real one. A family. And someone to put their hand on his back when the ghosts get too loud.

He doesn't need a pillow to fake affection anymore. He doesn't look for Christmas at the bottom of a drink. He found it — in laughter, in quiet mornings, in the warmth of people who show up and stay.

"So... this is Christmas?" he thinks again.

Yeah, kid. This is Christmas.

And you survived long enough to see it.

Now pour yourself a hot chocolate, hold someone you love, and be proud of the boy who made it out. Because that boy?

That boy was me.

# After the Lights Go Out

There's this moment — usually somewhere between the last bite of shortbread and the first garbage day of January — where everything just... dims. Not the lights strung across porches or the gaudy inflatables slouched in defeat on suburban lawns. I'm talking about the inside lights — the ones we try to keep lit with spiked eggnog, forced smiles, and half-hearted resolutions.

Yeah, I get a little sad when the holidays end. Sue me.

The world gets dressed up like it actually gives a damn — frosted rooftops, window displays, the scent of cinnamon trying its damnedest to mask the stench of burnt-out capitalism. And for a little while, just a flicker, people become soft again. We think of each other. We reach out. We call moms. We bake things we normally wouldn't. Even the jackasses at the grocery store seem slightly less homicidal.

For me, the magic isn't about Jesus or jingle bells — it's about her. My mother. She was at her best during the holidays. Alive in a way that made the world seem alright. Her kitchen smelled like hope and brown sugar, her laugh could overpower any storm cloud, and her presence was enough to make a boy feel like maybe — just maybe — everything would be okay.

And then she was gone.

So yeah, maybe the holidays are my last sacred connection to that feeling, to her. The music, the lights, the rituals... they stir up ghosts in a way that feels less like haunting and more like home.

But the new year doesn't give a shit about your grief. The calendar flips, the snow turns to grey slush, and suddenly the world forgets how to be gentle. It's back to emails, bills, cold coffee, and pretending to care about spring fashion. And just when you're trying to fake your way through January, grief swings by for another round: my sister, Lisa — three years gone this year. Doesn't even seem real. Feels like she just left, like I just blinked and missed her.

I know I sound like a walking Smiths album right now. I'm working on it. I really am.

People love the sun. They crave the heat, the patios, the illusion of joy you can bottle in sunscreen. Me? I've always been a fall guy. Give me sweaters and dying leaves. Give me a sky that matches my mood and a breeze that tells me to slow the hell down.

But maybe I've had it backward.

The present — that slippery, whispering little bastard — it's all we've got. The past is gone, sealed up in old Polaroids and perfume bottles you can't throw away. The future? It's just a rumor. A seductive lie told by calendars and self-help books.

And yet we live everywhere but here. We scroll, we reminisce, we worry, we wish. All while the now quietly slips through our fingers, like warm sand or the last good song on a road trip.

So maybe — just maybe — I start living here. Not in December. Not in September. But here. With whatever's in front of me. My wife's laugh. A perfectly steeped cup of tea. My dog snoring on the couch. A good fart joke. A bad rerun. A half-decent kiss at the right time.

Not a resolution. Just a vow.

To show up more. To look grief in the eye and say, "I see you, but I'm not giving you the whole day." To tell people I love them without needing a holiday as an excuse. To let the seasons pass without trying to live inside one of them.

So yeah, I'm a little less sad now than I was when I started writing this. Maybe that's the magic — turning sorrow into something you can hold, something that lets in a little light.

Happy New Year, friends. Here's to all of our messy, beautiful, complicated, present moments.

And hey — if you see me out there looking wistful come February, just know... I'm still chasing ghosts. But I'm doing it with both feet in the now.

# Until We Meet Again (and I Hope You Bring Scotch... Sorry... Water)

It's snowing again — that slow kind of fall that turns the world into a still life. No music. No chaos. Just the sound of your own breath and whatever regrets decide to pull up a chair. I should be doing something else — I don't know, stringing lights, wrapping gifts badly, making burnt toast for the kids just to see them laugh. But I'm here. With the ghosts.

You see, when it snows like this, I remember people.

Chris came to me the other night — not in a dream, not in some new-age incense-soaked séance — just a video game. One we used to play. Same old pixels, same dumb objectives. But this time, he wasn't there, yelling at me for rushing in like an idiot. I froze — not in the game, in real life — and set the controller down like it had just burned me. One tear. That's all. One stupid tear sliding down my face because the weight of "not enough time" suddenly outweighed everything else in the room. I never said thank you for saying yes every time I asked. And now, he's just silence between load screens.

Boomer, man... your death made Christmas hard. First one after we lost you felt like a holiday-themed apocalypse. Everyone drinking, laughing, talking nonsense — while I sat there with a smile so fake it could've been trademarked. They forgot you. Or maybe they didn't know how to remember. Either way, I drank enough scotch to try and forget for them. But I couldn't. Ever since the day my hand brushed the coffin they sealed you in, I've stopped letting joy in without first opening the door to grief. It's instinct now. Ritual. You before joy. Always.

Greg — the medic with a grin and the soul of a poet. You told me once this job wasn't a job. It was a calling. You meant it, too. Every word, wrapped in sincerity. So why the hell couldn't you answer your own call? Why'd you hang up on yourself? That one hurt in a new way — not like a punch, more like a slow knife you never saw coming. Christmas lights have flickered ever since, like they're not sure whether to shine or mourn.

Then there was Colin. God, Colin. You didn't just save me — you reminded me I was worth saving. I was coming apart at the seams, pretending to be a good soldier, a decent boyfriend, a son someone could be proud of. And there you were — "Hey, Henny," with that stupid lovable grin and that vibe that said, No need to pretend here, kid. You loved without conditions. Rare. Damn rare. You were my brother in ways biology could never touch.

And Starker... You were a human contradiction — all quiet storm and lethal calm. You scared the hell out of me when we met. Then you made me laugh until my stomach hurt. You could swear like a poet and hug like a bear. We weren't just soldiers, we were family. You taught me that blood doesn't mean much if there's no heart behind it.

And then there's Mum. You made Christmas weird and wonderful. Always did. You had a way of loving kids that was entirely your own — awkward, loud, imperfect. But it was love. And even now, when I watch the kids open their gifts, I still hear your off-key carols in the back of my mind. I wish you could see them. You'd be strange about it, but in the best way.

Lisa... my big sister. I saw you in the snow today. Just for a second. A flash of red in the white and gray outside my kitchen window. A trick of the light, probably. But I felt you. You always did love the snow. You'd hate how much I miss you. You always said I was too sentimental for my own good, but you never said it as an insult or judgement. You were right.

I want to call you all. I want to tell you about my life now — about the woman who fixed the cracks in my heart with nothing more than kindness and stubbornness, about the kids who taught me that joy isn't some mythical thing you chase — it's right here, in burnt toast, early morning cartoons, and sidewalk chalk on the driveway.

I'm four years sober. Imagine that. No flask, no bar stool, no Korean dive where the ghosts sit to my left and right. Just me, a warm house, a dog that snores like a chainsaw, and a heart that somehow still beats, still remembers, still loves.

I miss you all. Every damn day. But today — this snowy Tuesday that smells like pine and quiet — I miss you loud.

So here's to you — all of you. My ghosts. My brothers. My sister. My mother. You were the first ones to show me what love was, even if I didn't always recognize it at the time.

If I had one wish this Christmas, it wouldn't be for gadgets or toys or even a bestseller. I'd wish for one more drink with you — one more laugh, one more insult, one more quiet understanding that we were family, even when the world made no sense.

But since that's not on the menu, I'll sip my tea, stare out the window, and let the snow remember for me.

Merry Christmas. I love you. I remember you. And I'll keep the fire going until we meet again.

# Even the Green Ranger Gets Tired

Here's a cold, hard truth they don't put in comic books or Saturday morning reruns: your heroes? They're just people. Flesh and flaws. They bleed, they break, they ghost you without meaning to — or sometimes, forever. We grow up thinking capes are invincible. But eventually the cape comes off, and you're left staring at some guy in boots just trying to get through the day.

It's not the worst revelation in the world, but it sure as hell stings when one of your childhood titans taps out. Especially when they lose a fight to something invisible.

Jason David Frank — you might know him as that dude with the long hair and the roundhouse kick who wore green, then white, then green again. To me? He was the Green Ranger. And last night, I found out he's gone. Forty-nine. Suicide. And just like that, another one of my giants fell.

When I was a kid — and I mean the kind of kid who stared out the window like it owed him something — I didn't have much. No dad.

No safe landing. Just a stack of comic books, a static-filled TV screen, and the notion that someone, somewhere, could fight the bad and win. Superman. Batman. Daredevil. Buffy. Angel. And yeah, the damn Power Rangers. They weren't just characters. They were lighthouses. Beacons in the static.

I didn't have a dad, but Bruce Wayne didn't either, and that guy turned out all right. Sort of. I wasn't chiseled, I wasn't fearless, and I sure as hell wasn't in slow-motion martial arts montages. But every afternoon when that school bell rang, I ran home like salvation was airing at 4 o'clock. And it was.

Tommy Oliver — the Green Ranger — wasn't just another character. He was the underdog turned leader, the bad guy turned hero. He changed. That meant something to a kid like me. I watched him grow, struggle, lead. I watched him survive. So yeah, when I heard Jason David Frank didn't, it felt like a betrayal from the universe itself. Not him. Not that guy.

But that's the twist, isn't it? Even heroes have their demons. They just wear them differently. I should know. I've danced on the edge of the void myself — one foot over the rail, just me and my ghosts. I've lost people. Friends. Family. Too many to count. Suicide isn't some philosophical riddle to me — it's a bastard that shows up uninvited, drinks all your scotch, and leaves you with silence.

I don't judge anymore. I can't. I've seen too much, lost too much. My mother — gone. My sister — gone. Friends — gone. Judging would be like spitting on their graves. What I feel now isn't judgment. It's fatigue. It's grief. And yeah, it's love. Even if it's for someone I never met.

But I knew Tommy. That counts for something.

Those shows we called "kids' stuff"? They taught us more than most sermons and self-help books ever did. Be kind. Stand up. Fight for what's right. Don't lie. Tell the truth. Don't do drugs. Respect your elders. Believe in yourself, even when no one else does. That's not just screenwriting — that's survival training for broken kids.

Jason David Frank — Tommy — wasn't just a guy in spandex. He was a mirror, a map, a symbol. And losing him doesn't just hurt. It hollows.

But maybe that's the lesson. Heroes are human. They fall. They cry. They quit. And maybe — just maybe — that's what makes their light so important while it's here.

So what do we do?

We be kind. To ourselves, even when the mirror tells us we don't deserve it. To others, especially when they're being unkind — because that's usually when they need it most. We grow, with humility and bruised knees, and we understand that nobody gets through this life without a few scars. You're not broken because you're hurting. You're human.

This isn't about capes or color-coded costumes. This is about grace. This is about choosing love, again and again, even when it hurts. Especially when it hurts.

So to my childhood hero — the one who showed me you can start dark and still turn light — I say this:

Rest easy, Green Ranger.

You mattered.

And yeah... it's morphin' time.

# Hallways and Trailers

I had no idea what I was walking into. Not back then, and not yesterday. Funny how life doesn't give you warnings. No flashing lights, no musical score to let you know you're about to walk straight into the past disguised as the present.

Friday afternoon, snow drifting down like lazy regrets, I found myself meandering the hills of town toward a friend's place. A favor. Simple enough. "Can you check on the trailer while I'm out of town?" he'd asked. Of course, I said yes. That's what I do. That's who I am. I say yes before thinking. Before remembering.

It was supposed to be an in-and-out kind of thing. Lock up. Walk away. I've done far worse for people I care about far less.

The gravel driveway was long, uneven. The kind of road that has opinions about your tires. Something stirred in the back of my brain—soft, slippery, unnamed. But I didn't listen. Not really.

I got to the door. Fished for keys. First lock, then second. The door opened with that familiar trailer creak, and that's when the smell hit me. Subtle at first. The air had that metallic edge—copper and something sour. Blood-adjacent, like a memory trying to slip in unnoticed. But I brushed it off. Just bad air circulation or maybe a fridge left ajar.

Then I stepped inside.

To the left, a hallway stretched into the kind of shadow that doesn't just swallow light—it dares you to enter. And for reasons I can't explain, I did.

Around the corner, down the corridor—and boom.

Not a literal explosion. No fireball. No glass raining down like hail. Just that internal detonation. The kind your brain sets off when it recognizes a ghost before you do.

I wasn't in that trailer anymore. Not really. I was back. Different trailer. Different time. Same damn feeling.

The air turned thick, the walls pressed in. My pulse started auditioning for a prison break. I could feel the phantom weight of a flashlight in my hand. That night came rushing in like a flood: another trailer, another hallway, and a man who'd checked out before I even arrived. Half his face gone, the rest sprayed across the walls like some grotesque expressionist piece no gallery would dare hang.

They say not to look. But we always do.

The light from my flashlight had landed on his one good eye. Still open. Still staring. As if even he couldn't believe what he'd done. As if his body hadn't gotten the memo that this was the end. That eye haunts me more than the rest. It didn't just see me—it accused me. Of what, I don't know. Maybe of being too late. Maybe just of bearing witness.

Back in the present, I was still standing in my friend's hallway, but everything in me was somewhere else. Someone else. I couldn't breathe. Couldn't move. Then I bolted.

Outside, I collapsed onto a patch of cold, damp ground, like I was trying to dig my way back into the earth. My chest ached. My hands trembled. I begged my brain to let it go. It didn't listen.

I called Sheena. I don't remember what I said, just that I needed someone who knew how to speak my kind of broken. She showed up like she always does—calm, present, solid. I probably looked like hell. Felt like a kid who'd fallen off his bike one too many times, except there was no scraped knee to show her. Just a mess of invisible wounds and the wreckage of memory.

What's the moral of this story? Hell if I know. Maybe it's that trauma doesn't come with an expiration date. Just because you've put time and therapy between you and it doesn't mean it won't crawl back through the cracks.

Or maybe it's this: Don't check on trailers when your mind is a tripwire.

But the truth? I'll probably do it again. That's the curse of being dependable. Of being wired to help. Even if the house is on fire, you're the guy who walks in because someone asked nicely.

Life's messy like that. It's a grab bag of soft moments and sharp edges. You take the ugly with the beautiful and hope you land somewhere in the middle.

Yesterday was ugly. No sugarcoating that.

Today? Today's new. Today's quiet. I'll take it.

But for now, no more trailers. Not for a while.

"Life is what you make of it, and family is more than just blood — it's who you choose to love. So make something great and choose wisely."

—Matthew Heneghan

# CONTEMPLATION, CONVERSATIONS, AND OTHER THINGS

# That Beautiful Ballad Called Survival

So here we are — neck-deep in the chaos months. That stretch of calendar where birthdays butt up against holidays like drunk uncles at a family dinner. It's all candles and carols, deadlines and decorations, and somehow, despite it being the same every damn year, it still sneaks up behind us like a mugger in a dark alley. Boom — stress. Instant. Unapologetic.

And maybe you're feeling it. That squeeze in your chest, the calendar screaming louder than your alarm clock, the sense that you're already behind on a race you didn't know you entered.

So let me say this: You're doing your best. And most days, that's all the universe requires of you. Doesn't mean it'll all unfold the way you dreamt it up on a sleepy Sunday with good coffee and delusions of control — but it will work out. Eventually. Or at least it'll hurt less tomorrow. Sometimes, that's enough.

Take a second for yourself. Just one. Hell, take two if you're feeling rebellious. Breathe. Remind yourself that worth isn't something you earn — it's something you've had all along. And if you're anything like me, if self-worth feels like a pair of jeans two sizes too small, then borrow some belief from the people who see you differently. Trust them, even when you can't trust your own reflection.

You might not know me. I might not know you. But odds are, we've danced with some of the same demons. Different names, same playlists. That's the thing — we all carry stories, and most of them rhyme in places we don't talk about out loud. That's where empathy comes from. From that soft, bruised spot where we realize we're not alone.

So listen: I'm proud of you. Not in some Hallmark movie, overly-manicured kind of way. In the way that matters. You've had long days. Longer nights. You've weathered shitstorms and quiet breakdowns and probably smiled when you didn't mean it. But you're still here. Still breathing. Still putting one foot in front of the other, even if it's just to make coffee and collapse on the couch again.

Stress is a liar. It tells you that you're weak, that you're late, that you'll never make it. But you've made it before. You're stronger than your doubts give you credit for. Survivors always are.

So yeah, this is social media. Most days it feels more like a digital scream chamber than anything meaningful. But every now and then, it lets people reach each other across the noise. And if today you needed someone to remind you that you're doing alright — well, consider this me, extending a virtual cigarette and a crooked half-smile, saying: You've got this.

You're not alone. You're never alone.

With respect, sarcasm, and more belief in you than you probably have in yourself right now,

— Matthew.

# The Sun Sure is Bright

For most of my adult life, and maybe even some before, I hated the sun.

Not in that vampire, leather-coat-in-July kind of way. No, this was deeper. More visceral. It wasn't about skin or sweat or even heat. It was about memory. Tethers to more miserable times.

Hot days have a smell — you know the one; Asphalt cooking beneath your boots. The faint ozone buzz of electrical wires in a silent neighborhood. That orchestral sibilance of insect lamenting beneath blades of rusting grass. And more specifically to me... that sterile, suffocating stink of dried blood on pavement.

It all sticks to you.

I remember one summer afternoon — I remember it often — too hot for anything except bad decisions. We were called out for a code — boy, 14, suicide. We arrived just in time to do absolutely nothing. The kind of call where your hands still move, because that's what training demands, but your heart is already folding into itself like a dried leaf.

The sun that day was blinding. Indifferent. Unrelenting. It poured down on that scene like it wanted to bleach it clean. Like it couldn't stand to bear witness but didn't mind illuminating every painstaking detail for both my partner and I.

There were others.

The day I lost Colin. The morning I heard about Starker. Brothers I once served with; overseas, fighting someone else's war while I was knee-deep in ours — picking up addicts, suicides, the forgotten and the gone on the streets of my own weary city. The sun shone bright those days too, as if to say, "I see you." As if to ask, "Still think this is the better war?"

So, yeah. For a long time, I resented the hell out of it.

Give me cloud cover. Give me grey. Give me a sky that matches the way I feel inside and maybe I can find some goddamn peace. When I stopped drinking, all I wanted was rainfall. It was the only way for me to leave the goddamn house. Rain, a sad man's camouflage. Tears beneath raindrops.

But then something changed. Slowly. Like most good things do.

It started with golf, weirdly enough. My buddy Steven — a guy who somehow still believes mornings are for more than just hangovers — dragged me out onto the green one summer. Not to fix me. Just to hit things and laugh and say nothing important for a few hours. And wouldn't you know it? Somewhere between the swing and the silence, and my terrible slice, I felt... alright.

Then came the walks.

Golden hour. You ever notice how gentle the world gets just before the sun decides to call it a night? Like even the light knows it's time to stop being harsh. I started walking with friends — first thing in the morning before the sun remembers how hot it's supposed to be, or just before dusk. And for those brief windows, I don't hate it anymore. Footsteps in the company of kindness and pretty faces — it's a different kind of warmth a guy can really get used to.

Maybe it's age. Maybe it's therapy. Maybe it's just the soft exhaustion that comes after surviving a few too many things that should've taken you out. But I've started to let the sun back in. Bit by bit, ray by ray. I even manage a smile on those mornings when spears of sunlight spill in through the uneven slits of the blinds.

Turns out, it doesn't always have to mean death. Sometimes it means warmth. Sometimes it means quiet. Sometimes it just means you're still here to feel it, and that's a gift.

I used to think the sun was mocking me.

Now I think it's showing me the way to forgive. Both myself, and it.

If you'll please excuse me, I gotta go put some shades on. It's bright out here.

# Better Than Handsome

My mother once told me, "You're not going to be on the front of any magazine covers, but you could pass in a crowd. That's about as good as it gets."

Thanks, Mom.

I was maybe ten at the time, folded into the uncomfortable embrace of a faux-leather chair in some beige hospital room while she sat nearby, catching an IV drip like it was her job. Cancer had a way of making her sharp. Sharper than usual. I remember adjusting the coke-bottle lenses perched on my nose like they were a curse from a Greek tragedy. Or a comedy, depending on the lighting. She wasn't being cruel — just honest. Honest in the way only dying people and single mothers know how to be. She didn't believe in sugarcoating the world. She believed in surviving it. Or castigating it when it failed to meet her expectations.

And maybe she was right. I've never been handsome. Not in the kind of way that gets you out of parking tickets or onto the cover of GQ. I'm the kind of face you forget as soon as I leave the room. You don't remember my jawline — you remember my fuck-ups. I'm not photogenic, but my mistakes always seem to find the spotlight... or the back seat of a cop car on a muggy summer night.

Growing up, I thought glasses were the ultimate betrayal. Thick-rimmed proof that I wasn't that guy. You know the one — square-jawed, scruff in all the right places, eyes that could undress you and your trauma in one blink. I wanted to be him. Instead, I was the kid squinting through smudged lenses and prescription updates, hoping that charm could make up the difference.

Eventually, I leaned into it. I wore button-downs like armor. Let my hair grow until it looked like I might write something worth reading. Quoted Bukowski in the wrong bars to the wrong people. Told myself I was "worldly" or "interesting" — which is just what we say when we can't bring ourselves to admit we're not hot.

My older sibling once accused me of narcissism because I posted selfies online. Forgetting, conveniently, that for a lot of years I was alone in my company. I didn't post because I thought I was something. I posted because I hoped someone would tell me I was. That's not narcissism — that's insecurity dressed up in a 21st-century social ritual. And anyway, aren't we all just hoping someone sees us and doesn't flinch?

The thing about handsomeness is it's a lottery ticket. You either pull the right numbers or you don't. And if you don't, you learn to survive on scraps — wit, timing, empathy, damaged charm. You make people laugh. You write books. You tell stories that get stuck in the teeth of people's minds because they felt something, even if they don't remember your name.

Handsome fades. So does charming. So does everything, really. The older I get, the more I realize we're all just dressing up our insecurity and calling it personality.

If I'm not handsome, at least I'm observant.

But sometimes — sometimes — a woman looks at you like you're the only man in the room. And not because of your cheekbones, but because you see her too. Because in all the mess and mayhem and mediocrity, you made her feel something. You told the truth, and it was ugly, and broken, and hers.

That's better than handsome.

Hell, maybe that is handsome. In a way.

Or maybe it's just another lie I tell myself so I can walk out the front door without shame dragging me back inside by the collar.

In any case, I still haven't graced the covers of any magazine spreads. I'm still just trying to pass in a crowd.

And as my mum once said — maybe that's about as good as it gets.

# The Men Who Never Bleed

There's a scene in almost every bad barroom brawl I've ever witnessed: two idiots, puffed up on cheap whiskey and inherited trauma, chest-bump like rams in rutting season, each convinced they're the star in their own movie. One spills a drink, the other spills blood, and by the time the bartender calls the cops, nobody remembers what the fight was about. Just that someone was wronged somehow.

Now zoom out—way out—and that's geopolitics. A cosmic dick-measuring contest, played out with missiles, sanctions, and tweets written by men in suits who never bleed for the policies they write.

This time, it's the usual suspects: the U.S., Iran, and Israel. Three ancient egos on a global stage, all convinced that righteousness is theirs to define. That history is theirs to write. That consequences are for civilians and newspaper headlines.

And here we are again, watching the sparks from the same goddamn flint strike another fire.

Israel says they're defending their existence. Iran says they're defending their dignity. America says it's about peace, which is Washington code for, "Don't worry, we brought bigger guns." Somewhere in a press room, a man in a tie and dead eyes will call it a "measured response." Somewhere else, a child will die from it.

It's always the people who didn't vote for the fight who pay for it. Funny how that works.

Ego is the quiet engine of history. It's Alexander and Caesar and Churchill and Nixon and Netanyahu and whoever's whispering to whichever political figurehead is in office today. It's the inability to back down, even when the cost is measured in mothers who have to identify their sons by their dental records.

Cheques are written in blood and cashed in by those that die young.

I used to believe that writing could change things. That a well-placed sentence could slow the march toward madness. Now I'm not so sure. These days, I write more like a man scratching his last words into a prison wall — not because anyone's going to read them, but because silence would be a lie.

I don't know what the end looks like. But I've read enough books and witnessed enough wreckage to know how it usually starts.

It starts with pride. With men too afraid to be seen blinking. With old grudges dressed in new uniforms. With a lie big enough to fit on a flag and small enough to chant in a crowd.

The missiles are already in the air. The headlines are already written. And somewhere in the noise, someone will say, "This was necessary."

But I've been alive long enough to know one thing:

War isn't about necessity. It's about men with unresolved father issues and god complexes trying to outrun their own reflection while thinking they know what's best.

And they'll always find a way to bring the rest of us along for the ride.

# Not Weak... Wounded

I once met an old retired paramedic who said, "PTSD? I don't even know what that is. You can either handle it or you can't."

Yesterday on the golf course, I met a former volunteer firefighter. Midway through a casual chat, he said, "Yeah... tough job being a firefighter or medic. Some people just can't handle it."

I've heard variations of that phrase before, and I'll say this plainly:

I vehemently oppose this concept.

PTSD isn't about who's tough or who's soft. It's not a character flaw. It's not weakness.

It's about exposure.

It's about repeated injury to the mind and heart. About walking into chaos when everyone else is running out. About witnessing the worst moments of people's lives — and still showing up again tomorrow. And the next day. And the next.

I've seen the toughest men and women break down after years of running calls that would traumatize anyone. That doesn't mean they 'couldn't handle it' — it means they did, over and over, until their nervous system simply said, 'enough.' PTSD is often the delayed invoice of prolonged endurance.

It's not the broken who suffer trauma. It's the human. The compassionate. The ones who offer pieces of themselves to others in hopes that others may live. Or the ones who sit, silently taking in what just happened. The ones who go home and sit quietly in the dark, because they don't want to burden their families with the weight of what they saw.

PTSD doesn't mean you couldn't handle it.

It means you did.

You handled it until it started handling you.

We don't need more people bragging about being unfazed. We need more people brave enough to admit that they were — and still found the courage to heal.

# Lessons from Berk

Last night I watched How to Train Your Dragon — the live-action version. Never saw the original. I wasn't exactly a Dreamworks-and-popcorn kind of guy before Sheena came into my world. Kids weren't in my orbit, and let's face it, dragons weren't either. But there I was, a 42-year-old man sitting on a worn theatre seat, watching animated mythology come to life — and somehow, I walked away feeling like I'd just seen a goddamn sermon. In a good way.

Here's the setup: dragons and humans have been butting heads since time immemorial. Fire, death, swords — the works. But one kid, the protagonist, starts asking the forbidden question: Why?

Why are we fighting?

Why are we so hell-bent on keeping up the blood feud?

Why does it feel safer to cling to the fight than to drop the sword?

And that's when it hit me — somewhere between a dragon's roar and a silent, smoky stare-off — this wasn't a kid's movie. It was a mirror made of profound glass and lesson.

Because the truth is, we're not that different from the Vikings and dragons on screen. We're all just dragging our old wounds around like badges of honour. Entire identities built on grievance. Like if we let go of the hurt, we lose the only thing that gives us shape. And yeah — letting go is terrifying. Because then who are we, if not a wronged party? If not the victim?

That movie didn't end with revenge. It didn't demand reparations. Nobody stood at a podium and screamed, You owe me. Nobody turned their pain into political currency. They just stopped. Looked. Listened. And they chose something else — peace. Not the naïve, fairy-tale kind. The earned kind. The kind you reach when you realize the fight is no longer worth the bruises.

Now, I'm not foolish enough to say real life is just a movie waiting for a happy ending. I know better. The world's messy. Politics are ugly. Trauma is real. But so is ego. So is entitlement. And those things? They're the gasoline we keep pouring on already smoldering fires. We call it justice, but half the time it's just pride wearing a halo, or false narratives spoken on words of virtue.

I guess what I'm saying is this: dragons didn't start the war. Humans did. But the younger generations born on the isle of Berk had only ever known one thing — the violence of dragons. And then one human had the guts to admit it was all bullshit.

Maybe that's the kind of bravery we need today.

Not louder voices, not hotter takes — just quieter questions.

Why are we still fighting?

What are we really defending?

And what would it cost to just let go?

Not everything needs to be settled. Sometimes, healing doesn't come with a courtroom or a cheque. Sometimes, it starts when someone drops the sword first.

Yeah, I watched a dragon movie. And yeah, it kicked me right in the soul. So be it.

Anyway, essentially what I am saying, is that it was a great movie!

# The Rule of Law According to Mac & Cheese

Time is a goddamn illusion. That's what I've decided. A cruel, cosmic prank. You start the day with the best of intentions — a tidy to-do list, maybe even a little optimism — and before you know it, the sun's going down and all you've got to show for it is a stubbed toe, two missed calls, and a dinner plan that's devolved into boxed macaroni and a prayer.

There's probably some celestial asshole up there laughing his ethereal ass off while we mortals hustle to beat the clock. Spoiler: we never do.

And here's the kicker — the world doesn't fall apart when we don't get it all done.

Maybe you're late. So what? Apologize. Blame traffic or time dilation or the existential weight of modern life. Whatever. The point is, most of the time, it doesn't matter. You're not curing cancer — you're picking up dry cleaning and trying to remember if you fed the dog.

Dinner plans fizzle? Congratulations, you've just rediscovered the guilty comfort of powdered cheese and overcooked pasta. Miss the movie? They're showing it again tomorrow. Hell, they'll probably reboot it in five years anyway — with worse casting.

Today, I forgot the meat in the freezer. Left the house twice without my wallet. Stubbed my toe so hard I considered writing it a eulogy. I was late picking up the kids, again. And yeah, I felt like a bit of a failure — a walking, talking, slightly limping cautionary tale.

But here's the thing: I'm still here. Still standing. Well, wobbling. But upright.

We don't break as easy as we think. Life doesn't give a damn about our lists or our schedules. It just keeps coming, like a drunk text at 2 a.m. — unpredictable, often irritating, occasionally profound.

So breathe. Burn the list. Make peace with the mac & cheese.

You're not behind. You're just human.

And that? That's enough.

# Mother's Day, But... Sheena

Ah, Mother's Day. A day that, historically, has carried with it a certain heft of melancholy.

On one hand, it ties me to thoughts of my own mother. I miss her. I never knew—nor would I have ever suspected—that Mother's Day of 2016 would be the last time I'd get to wish her well, or send her flowers.

But on the other side of that sadness, I have Sheena. A sterling example of motherhood in all its beautiful complexity. That woman never ceases to amaze me. Her ability to juggle the near-limitless tasks of being a mother, a business owner, and a spouse is nothing short of extraordinary.

Life with my mother was... complicated. And as such, the day dedicated to mothers often felt heavy—clouded and nerve-inducing.

But Sheena has changed that for me. She's brought clarity and warmth to a day that once felt so conflicted. Now, this humble square on the calendar has become something to look forward to. A day to pause, reflect, and show just how grateful we are to have such wonderful women in our lives.

Sheena, happy Mother's Day. Thank you for letting me walk beside you in this wild and beautiful journey.

I love you—to the moon, and back... and then some.

# Fairway Therapy and Egg Salad

What do you get when you mix egg salad sandwiches, cold drinks, and acres of pretentious lawn cut with military precision — all served with a side of banter from a friend who knows where the bodies are buried?

You get therapy. The good kind. The kind they don't bill you for.

Sure, it sounds dramatic — but I'm a writer. Melodrama is my bread and butter. And sometimes, egg salad.

It was one of those weeks. The kind where your to-do list stares back at you like it knows it's going to win. Bills, burnout, deadlines — the holy trinity of adulthood. So when Steven rolled up to my place like some denim-clad golf chariot, I took the hint: we needed out.

Out of our heads, out of town, and onto the green. Or, in our case, slightly adjacent to it — usually in the rough, occasionally in the woods, once in a pond. But that's not the point.

We didn't bother with warm-up swings or stretching routines. We're not athletes. We're aging men with good intentions and bad knees. We hopped in the cart, cracked a cold one, (mine was a soda) and rode off into the afternoon like two cowboys who traded in their horses for a four-wheeled puttering steed.

Swoosh. Smack.

The first drive was clean. Honest. A small miracle in a world full of slices and regrets.

Golf is stupid. A rich man's curse. A poor man's fantasy. It's also painfully poetic. You line up a shot with all the confidence of a Greek god, only to watch your ball hook left like it owes someone money. But you keep swinging. Because sometimes — once in a blue moon — the shot soars. And you remember why you keep coming back.

It's life, really. You tee up with the best of plans, only to land two inches from a pinecone and a hornet's nest. You curse. You improvise. You laugh because if you don't, you cry. And the only thing that makes the whole mess bearable is the guy riding shotgun. The friend who tells you your backswing looks like a drunken flamingo, but still hands you a sandwich like you just won the Masters.

Steven — good man, better friend — brought the sandwiches. Egg salad. Homemade. Not some sad grocery store mashup with a plastic lid. No, this was comfort food on soft bread, handed to me somewhere between hole six and existential reflection.

Was it dumb to feel peace while chewing egg salad in the sun? Maybe. But peace doesn't need to make sense. Sometimes it just shows up in the form of sunshine, birdies, and the occasional "what the hell was that swing?" from a guy who's seen you at your best and your worst.

So yeah, golf. Stupid, beautiful, infuriating golf. Thank God for it.

Here's to a straight drive, a good lie, and a quiet afternoon where everything — just for a little while — makes perfect sense.

And may the sandwiches always be fresh, my friend.

# Salmon Arm & Other Ghost Stories

Ever get sucker-punched by a memory? Not the kind you chase, but the kind that stalks you quietly until it finds the perfect moment to leap out and remind you that your past has claws? That was me this weekend — all dressed up, politely clapping at a writers' gala, while ghosts took turns jabbing me in the ribs.

I was the guest of honour. Fancy, right? First place for a nonfiction piece. Got the email and everything. Big deal, apparently. The gala was held in Salmon Arm — which, despite sounding like a failed seafood dish, is actually a real town. My town. Or at least it used to be. Back before life got complicated and nostalgia turned into a game of Russian roulette.

See, memory's not a friend. It's an ex that keeps showing up uninvited. Sometimes drunk. Sometimes sweet. But always with an agenda.

I was standing there — awkwardly elegant in a borrowed blazer — when I heard a voice call my name. I turned, smiled politely, and locked eyes with a woman I didn't recognize... until I did.

Flashback: Me, nine years old, tossed around like unwanted luggage because my mom was too tired, too sick, or just too done to deal with me. I'd be "shipped out" to random acquaintances — people I didn't know but apparently knew me. Overnight bags packed with blind optimism. One pair of socks, one comic book, and a deep-rooted sense of being in the way.

This woman — standing in front of me now with wine in hand and kindness in her eyes — was one of those adults. I'd stayed at her house. I remembered her daughter, Sasha. Sweet kid. Down syndrome. We were the same age, but worlds apart. She had a circle of friends. I was just a visitor. A misplaced puzzle piece left on someone else's kitchen table.

And now here she was, smiling and making small talk like we were old pals, while I stood there wondering how many of my childhood memories involved wearing someone else's clothes because I'd outstayed my welcome and no one thought to pack more underwear.

I brushed it off. Politely. Maybe even convincingly. But internally? Strike one.

Then we found our table, and I was gearing up to relax when I heard it again — my name, but softer this time. Like someone stepping on a landmine with good intentions.

I turned and there she was: Jordan's mom.

Jordan. Hockey teammate. Decent shot. Great kid. One of the few who didn't treat me like I was radioactive. I remembered his mom. She was one of the parents who bought me food after games when everyone else had combo meals and I had invisible shame. I'd always say, "I'm not hungry." Which was code for "I'm broke." And she always knew. Always offered anyway. No questions, just fries and quiet dignity.

Now here she was, decades later, pulling that memory out of me like a magician's handkerchief — only this one was soaked in guilt and old grease from a fast-food joint off the highway. Strike two.

See, it's not that I'm ungrateful. I'm the opposite of ungrateful. I remember every act of kindness, every quiet mercy that helped me survive growing up on government cheese and broken promises. It's just... when you live with shame long enough, it becomes less of a feeling and more of a reflex. Even now, surrounded by applause and accolades, it finds a way to sit beside me, whispering, "Do they know?"

Salmon Arm — town with a dumb name and a hold on my ribcage. It's small enough for people to remember you, but just big enough for you to forget who you were. Or maybe try to.

The gala was lovely. The food, fine. The speeches? Mercifully short. But I couldn't shake the weight. Not because of them. Because of me. Because memory, for people like us, is rarely just a stroll down a golden lane — it's a goddamn minefield. And some of us are just trying to walk through it with both legs still attached.

So yeah, I won something. Cool. But I also revisited the ruins. And I'm still trying to figure out if that makes me brave... or just stupid.

Maybe both.

Salmon Arm — still haunted. Still home. Sort of.

# Virgin Mojitos & Other Stupid Ideas

Why do we do it?

Why do we break our backs and bruise our egos trying to be everything for everyone? Who was the first poor bastard to look at a room full of people and think, "Yeah, I got this. I can make them all like me." Probably someone with a nice smile and crippling anxiety. Probably someone like me. Or you.

We come into this world sticky, screaming, and completely dependent — and from that first breath, we're already performing. Cry to get picked up. Smile to get fed. Be agreeable so people don't leave. And it only gets worse from there. Somewhere along the way, we start mistaking likability for survival. As if being liked is the rent we pay to exist.

But here's the punchline: trying to please everyone is like trying to make a virgin mojito taste good. No matter how much mint you cram in the glass, it's still just fancy lime water pretending to be fun. And you? You're the bartender stuck faking joy while drowning in citrus.

You want the truth? Nobody makes it out of life liked by everyone. Hell, you could hand out gold bars on a street corner and someone would still complain they're too heavy. People are weird like that.

And sure, people with big hearts are the ones who get caught in this trap the most. The helpers. The givers. The "I'll-be-there-no-matter-what" types. You want to be generous? Be generous. But don't bleed yourself dry trying to fill someone else's cup. Even airplanes figured that out — put on your own damn mask first.

We glorify self-sacrifice, but forget that martyrs usually end up dead. Or, at the very least, bitter. And bitter ain't noble — it's just exhausted wrapped in resentment.

So, draw the damn line. Help where you can, not where you're expected to. Love without conditions. Give without gutting yourself. And when the world starts making noise about how you "owe" them something for your kindness, smile politely... and pour yourself something cold. Maybe even that virgin mojito — just to remind yourself how ridiculous it is to pretend everything needs to please everyone.

You're not a drink order. You're not a committee's consensus. You're a human being with finite energy and an infinite list of people who will never get you.

And that's okay.

So breathe. Take your mask. Sip your terrible faux cocktail. And get on with your life.

The real ones will still be there — even if the mojito sucks.

# The Forecast Calls for Melancholy

There's something quietly poetic about the sky when it decides to throw a tantrum. One minute, it's all bright blue serenity — like a promise it has no intention of keeping — and the next, it's brooding, sullen, heavy with unshed tears. Sounds familiar, doesn't it? Like life. Like us.

I've always had a thing for the rain. Not the stormy, end-of-days kind — but the soft, steady drizzle that taps at your window like an old friend who doesn't need to be let in. The kind of rain that doesn't ask for attention but gets it anyway. It doesn't demand anything. It just is. And in a world full of people screaming to be seen, that's refreshing.

There's peace in it. Real peace. Not the kind you find in overpriced yoga studios or those apps that try to fix your insomnia with whale sounds. I'm talking about the kind that slips in uninvited, wraps around your ribs, and whispers, "It's okay. You can stop pretending now."

Rain doesn't care about your deadlines or your bad decisions. It doesn't care who ghosted you or why you're still checking your ex's Instagram like it's a crime scene. Rain is just there, doing its thing — reminding you that everything, even pain, gets diluted eventually.

It's funny — rain makes the world smaller. Closer. A city that usually shoves you aside suddenly invites you to take your time. People stop sprinting toward nothing and start moving like they've actually got hearts in their chests. Even the usual suspects — the umbrella-duelists, the newspaper shield-bearers, the ones with coffee cups and chaos in their eyes — slow down. Some even smile. Or maybe their lips twitch with something that almost resembles hope.

Maybe that's why I love it. Because rain doesn't lie. It doesn't fake the sunshine. It just comes, unapologetically, soaking everything — especially the parts of you you thought were safe. And when it leaves, it doesn't say goodbye. It just fades out like the last note of a sad song, leaving behind something cleaner, clearer.

We all need a good rinse now and then — a cosmic reset. And no, I'm not saying rain fixes everything. I'm not that guy. I'm just saying it gives you a moment. A pause. A breath. And sometimes that's enough.

So here's to the rain — the sky's way of telling us to shut up, sit down, and feel something. Let it fall. Let it wash. Let it remind you that even the storm has somewhere else to be.

And maybe, just maybe, you'll find yourself humming some tune you thought you forgot... and realizing, for once, you're not in such a hurry to stop the downpour.

# Closing Time for Lonnie

Bars are cathedrals for the damned. Sanctuaries of second chances, slurred apologies, and hollow declarations of "just one more." Under the soft flicker of neon and the chorus of glass meeting glass, the oldest lie in the world is whispered over and over: This time will be different.

It never is.

Alcohol is a charming bastard. Shows up dressed to the nines, full of promise and punchlines, but leaves with your dignity, your health, and half the people you ever gave a damn about. I should know. I've danced with that devil — barefoot and unbalanced — more times than I care to admit. And I've watched it chew up better men than me. One of those men was Lonnie.

We met in a rehab circle, which, if you've never had the pleasure, is like speed dating in hell. Sad stories for small talk, trauma as currency. Lonnie was a bricklayer. Hands like sledgehammers, a voice like gravel soaked in whiskey, and a heart somewhere deep beneath the callouses and nicotine. His vocabulary had two settings: blunt and blunter — most of it punctuated with "fuck," "fuckin'," and "fuckin' right." But if you listened past the ashtray and drywall dust, you'd hear the good in him. He meant well. He just said it like he was starting a bar fight.

After rehab, we kept in touch. Not often, but enough. East coast to west, mostly online — the digital equivalent of two old barflies trading stories across a cracked vinyl booth. Every few weeks, I'd get a message saying he was banned from Facebook again for some half-baked rant or graphic meme. He was proud of it. I was proud of him.

I mailed him a copy of my book once — inscribed it, even. Sent him a military patch for that beat-up backpack he was always flexing in his photos. He thanked me. Said he was excited to read it. That was the last real exchange we had. I didn't know it'd be the last. But maybe I should have. That's the thing about this life — the endings aren't always surprises. Sometimes they're slow fades we refuse to look at.

A few weeks back, I realized I hadn't seen Lonnie post anything in a while. No rants. No steaks. No blurry selfies with his dog. I searched his name. Found the post. You know the kind. A mutual friend fumbling with words, announcing to the world that another one of us didn't make it. Just... didn't make it.

"Shocked.... friends in high school... rest in eternal peace."

That was it.

I stared at the screen like maybe it had more to say. Like maybe if I waited long enough, Lonnie himself would reply, telling me it was just another one of his bans. But it wasn't.

In rehab, they tell us this'll happen. That you'll lose people. That the guy sitting next to you in group could be a ghost by next month. You nod like you understand. But you don't. Not really. Not until your tea goes cold while you're staring into the void of a Facebook memorial.

Lonnie lived hard, unapologetically, without pretense or polish. He didn't care for small talk. Didn't fake smiles. He grilled like a pro, cursed like a sailor, and treated friendship like an unspoken pact: say what you mean, mean what you say, and fuck the rest.

So here's to you, Lonnie — my calloused, gravel-throated, heart-on-his-sleeve comrade in recovery. Thank you for the gallows humour in group, the late-night chats, the reminders that even broken men can build something solid.

Wherever you are — I hope the grill's hot, the coffee's strong, and no one's flagging your posts.

It's closing time, brother.

And you always hated long goodbyes.

# Lonnie Was Not the Last

Addiction — it's like a storm on the horizon. A thick, black cumulonimbus rolling in slow and mean, promising ruin. You can squint at the sky and pretend it's just overcast, that the sun's just behind the clouds. You can lie to yourself and say you're fine. But storms don't care if you believe in them. They don't negotiate.

You will get wet.

I did.

So did Ashton.

It was the summer of 2018, and I was several weeks into my voluntary incarceration at Berkshire Centre for Addictions and Trauma. The kind of place that promises peace and clarity but trades in broken people and cold institutional tar passing as coffee. That's where I met him — Ashton. A name you could find in any phone book, but a presence you didn't forget.

He was kind. The sort of kind that gets you bullied in high school and ignored at parties. Soft around the eyes, with glasses too big for his face. Not Coke-bottle thick like mine, but substantial enough to say, "Hey, I read more than I talk." He looked like the human version of an owl — not insultingly, but curiously. Thoughtful. Hesitant. Watchful. The kind of guy who thinks before he speaks, then thinks again, and ends up saying nothing at all.

His voice was shy, fragile. Like it was afraid to take up space. In groups, he'd hover near the edge of a thought, then retreat before finishing it. Unless he knew you. If he trusted you, if you earned a place in his quiet circle, you'd get glimpses — of wit, of insight, of someone who noticed things most people missed.

Somehow, I got let into that circle.

One afternoon I found him hunched over a table in the common room. A dictionary and thesaurus cracked open in front of him like dissected animals.

"Whatcha doing, Ash?" I asked, biting into an apple.

He looked up like a kid caught cheating on a test. "Me? Nothing. Just... working on my goodbye speech."

I grinned. "Goodbye? What, you planning to off yourself? If so, can I have your X-Box?"

He smirked. "No. I mean, yes — you can have my X-Box. But, no, I am not suiciding." Suiciding — bold use of a noun as a verb. "I'm just trying to write this stupid speech. I don't even... fucking hell." He snapped the dictionary shut and tossed his pen like it had insulted his mother.

"What's up?" I asked, my joking tone fading.

He mumbled something I couldn't catch. I waited.

"I don't want to leave," he said finally, voice shaking.

"What do you mean — you don't want to leave Berkshire?"

He nodded. "There's nothing out there. I have friends here. People are nice here. Like you."

The simplicity of it nearly broke me. He called me "nice." I'd spent years trying to be good, or at least look like I was. I never imagined anyone would hand me that word without conditions.

"Thanks, buddy," I said. "People are nice to you because you're a good guy. Solid dude."

He shook his head. "People are nice in here. Not out there. Not in the real world."

And there it was — the truth underneath his hesitation, the root of his fear. Outside these walls, Ashton was a misfit. He didn't fit the boxes. He didn't come with social armor or irony or Instagram polish. He was just Ashton. Earnest, awkward, kind. And the world eats people like that alive.

Inside Berkshire, we were all damaged goods. No pretense. No small talk. Just shared suffering, group therapy, and awkward hugs. You didn't have to explain why you were sad. Everyone just got it. It was a safe zone, a rare place where no one judged you for bleeding.

I think for Ashton, it might've been the only place he ever felt safe. Ever felt seen.

We sat there for a while, my apple forgotten. I tried offering what little wisdom I had — the kind cobbled together from war stories and therapy worksheets. He mostly just stared at the table, lost in thoughts too heavy to lift.

"You worried about drinking again?" I asked.

He looked up. "I'm worried I'll never have friends again."

That line hit me in the chest with the weight of a prolonged coronary. No drama. No tears. Just cold, devastating honesty. And he meant it. You could see it in his face — he believed it.

I gave him the usual reassurances. You'll find your people. You're not alone. But even as I said the words, I could tell they landed like wet matches. No spark.

We had a session to get to, so I let him be.

The next morning, he stood at the podium with his goodbye speech. Except he didn't look proud or ready. He looked like someone being forced onto a plane he knew would crash. Slumped shoulders. Blank face. You learn to recognize that look when you've worn it yourself.

He read his speech — nervous, wavering, sincere. He said he didn't want to go. That if it were up to him, he'd pay rent to Berkshire just to stay in his little room with the calming beige walls and the broken lamp he'd somehow fixed. The line was meant to be a joke, but the way he looked up after he said it — like he was hoping someone would say yes — was gutting.

He shook my hand afterward and promised to keep in touch.

"You still owe me that X-Box," I said.

He smiled. "You'll get it."

Months passed. I got out, started the slow, clumsy dance of reintegration. Learning how to exist in a world without booze. Without a buffer. Without the chemical crutch I'd used to silence the ghosts of military service and trauma and childhood grief.

One night in January, my phone buzzed.

"Hey. You awake?"

I didn't recognize the number, but I knew the voice behind the text.

"Ashton! Still up? I'm having a late-night tea. You?"

"Yeah. No tea."

There was a pause — fifteen, maybe twenty minutes.

Then: "Do you think one drink is okay? Like, if I'm shaking and stuff?"

My stomach turned.

"If you're shaking, you should go to the hospital, man. That's the safest place."

Another pause.

"I have a drink here... should I drink it?"

Addicts do this — look for permission, for some absolution. If someone else says it's okay, then maybe it won't hurt so bad.

"No," I told him. "Don't."

That was the last text of the night.

Two weeks later, another message.

"Hey."

"Ashton! You good?"

"I hate to ask..."

"Ask what?"

"I just need some money until mine comes in. I'll pay you back. I promise."

"I'm sorry, man. I can't. I just can't."

"Okay. Thanks anyway."

That was it. That was our last conversation. I didn't hear from him again.

Not until February 3rd, 2019. My birthday.

A friend of his texted me.

Ashton had been found dead in his apartment.

Gone.

Addiction doesn't care if you're kind. Doesn't care if you're funny, or lonely, or full of promise. It doesn't care if you're Ashton. It just wants more.

One more bottle.

One more pill.

One more life.

One more anything to fill the hole.

I read his obituary. Clicked the link to the memorial page. Saw photos of him as a kid, in pajamas with skiers on them. A Teenage

Mutant Ninja Turtles shirt I swear I had too. There were pictures of him in crowds, surrounded by people, smiling. He was never as alone as he thought he was.

But depression doesn't care about facts. It cares about feelings. And Ashton felt alone. That's what killed him.

I wish I had told him what he meant to me. That he helped me get through some dark days just by being himself. Not by giving speeches or saving lives. Just by being there. By being Ashton.

Born March 16, 1985. Died February 3, 2019.

There's a void where he used to be. Not just in my phone or my memory, but in the world. In the space where quiet kindness used to sit, quietly holding everything together without ever demanding credit.

Here's to you, Ashton.

May your name be said with reverence. May your story outlive the silence that took you. And may the world treat the next Ashton a little more kindly.

Thank you, my friend.

Thank you.

# Garbage Day Wisdom

Tuesdays and Thursdays. Where I'm from, we don't call them that. We call them garbage days.

This morning, I shuffled out the front door, half-dressed and half-awake, into the oppressive heat of a summer that had already overstayed its welcome. The sky looked hungover. So did I. The bin was full, as it always is. One hand on a bloated black bag, the other swatting away a cloud of ambitious flies. And then, somewhere between the driveway gravel and the street, it hit me — the poetry of it all.

Garbage day. The unsung ritual of starting over.

Every week, we drag our refuse to the curb. We let strangers take it from us. We never ask where it goes, just that it's gone by morning. That's trust. That's release. That's letting go.

Funny how we don't think twice about tossing out spoiled milk or an expired pizza box. But try doing the same with an old photo album or a toxic relationship and suddenly everyone gets philosophical. We clutch things long past their prime — objects, stories, people. We confuse guilt for love and nostalgia for necessity.

The truth? Most of what we carry, we don't need.

We hold onto broken things because we're afraid of forgetting. Or worse, being forgotten. But memories don't live in stuff. They live in us. And there's a fine line between holding on and hoarding.

Not everything is meant to be kept. That sweater you haven't worn since the breakup? Let it go. The box of mismatched buttons, lost charger cables, and old birthday cards? Toss it. The person who drains you more than they fill you? Same rules apply.

Letting go isn't an act of cruelty. It's mercy — for yourself, mostly. It's acknowledging something's run its course. That it served its purpose, and its purpose isn't now.

I'm not suggesting we forget the past. Just that we stop living in it. Every object we cling to, every "what if" we tuck away on a shelf, takes up space we could be using for something better. Something real. Something now.

Life's messy enough without dragging yesterday's junk into tomorrow.

The past will always exist. But it doesn't have to exist here.

We don't talk enough about emotional clutter. We glorify the hoard. We slap sentimental value on everything and call it meaningful. But sometimes meaning is knowing when to part ways.

Take it from me. I've kept things too long. People, too. And when you keep things past their usefulness, they don't just rot — they rot you.

There's dignity in walking someone or something to the metaphorical curb and whispering, "Thanks... but that's enough now."

You're not cruel for outgrowing someone. You're not heartless for choosing peace. You're human. And humans are designed to grow. Even weeds grow. So don't shame yourself for choosing sunlight.

Today, I set my bin out like I always do. And maybe I tossed more than just garbage. Maybe I let go of a little guilt. A little shame. A few things I've been carrying too long, convincing myself I had to.

And the world didn't end.

Maybe that's the secret. Let go, and trust that someone — or something — will take it from there.

Happy garbage day.

Here's to getting lighter.

# Puffy Little Miracles

To fight the bad things — the claws of memory, the restless ghosts that tap on the inside of your skull when the world's too quiet, I try to find beauty in the little things. Not the headline stuff. Just the everyday miracles most people walk past. Like this morning. I hadn't slept much. That fragmented kind of sleep that leaves your brain fogged and your heart heavier than it has any right to be. I got out of bed because staying in it felt like drowning. I wandered to the window, tugged the blinds just enough to peer through, and stood there like some hollowed-out version of myself, watching night surrender to day.

That's when I saw them — the clouds.

Swollen, slow-moving, indifferent to everything. Ink-blotted across a bruised sky, like they were dragged there by something older than time. Then, without ceremony, light began to creep in. Just a suggestion at first. A whisper of warmth across the horizon. Then came the marigold. The amber. The honey. The kind of color that doesn't show off but still takes your breath away.

And in that moment, something in me softened.

I stood there watching light overtake dark, as it always seems to do, and I let the silence fill me up. It was a small thing; clouds at dawn. But it was mine. A tether to the present. And sometimes, that's all you get.

Because there are days (too many, honestly) when the past doesn't stay in the past. When it crawls out of the cracks and pulls you under without warning.

She was four months old.

That detail never stops cutting. Never dulls. I'd been a paramedic for years, seen things that would gut most people. But that day? That one folded itself into me in a way nothing else ever had.

She was lying on her back on the couch, in a pink onesie that stabbed into my eyes and stapled itself to my memory. No visible injuries, no warning, no sound — just stillness. Her family stood frozen in the quiet chaos of their living room, and we stepped in like we always did, trying to rewind time with our hands.

We worked her. Fluids. Tubes. Compressions. I knelt beside her until my knee throbbed, until sweat clung to my spine, until I'd used everything I knew and still got nothing back. No pulse. No cry. Not a whimper. Just silence.

There's a certain kind of stillness that's louder than any scream. I've lived in it.

That morning, when I got out of bed, that same knee flared up... a reminder. My body remembering what my heart can't forget. I carry that moment in my bones. And for a long time, I tried to drink it away. Whiskey was my way out. Enough of it, and the world blurred into something quieter. Something black and merciful. No memories. No pink onesie. Just a void to curl up in.

But voids aren't homes. They're just hiding places.

Now, I look for beauty instead. I look at the way Sheena smiles when she thinks no one's watching. The way the girls laugh like they've never met fear. I look at the sky, and the way morning refuses to stay gone. I remember that even the darkest night has an ending. Even grief has its edges worn down by time and tenderness.

There's beauty in clouds, even when my chest feels hollow. Even when I ache. Even when the past drags its teeth across my ribs. And that beauty doesn't erase the pain, but it gives it company. It gives it shape. It tells me I'm still here, and I still feel.

I used to drink to forget. Now, I remember so I don't have to.

Because day always overtakes night. Slowly. Quietly. Without asking for applause.

And that, somehow, is enough.

# When the Sirens Come Calling

Sirens have a way of splitting my world in half. One moment, it's just another lazy rural morning, all birdsong and breeze. The next, that melody gets torn apart by the wail of something urgent, something metallic and mournful. That's when the present starts to flicker. Like a scratched film reel. Gone.

And just like that, I'm not here anymore.

Smoke. That's what it feels like — my grasp on the now, evaporating before I even knew I was holding it.

That's PTSD for you. It doesn't knock. Doesn't ask permission. It just shows up, uninvited and unapologetic, dragging you back to places you never wanted to see again.

And me? I go. I have to.

Back to the street corners slick with someone's blood. Back to living rooms filled with screams and disbelief. Back to the back of an ambulance, where the lights flash like some cruel disco while you pound on a chest and lie through your teeth, saying it's gonna be okay.

It's a strange job — being a medic. It's playing God without the power. Carrying people's lives in your hands while knowing you might not be enough. And when you lose... you don't just walk away. You carry it.

Forever.

There are things you learn in that job. Things no textbook could ever teach. The sound a mother makes when her child stops breathing. The weight of a body that's just transitioned from living to not. The way eyes go wide and then... nothing. It becomes routine. Which is its own kind of horror.

Some days, I hate the sirens. Most days, if I'm being honest. But here's the twist — I also miss them. I miss the rush. The way your blood starts sprinting before your mind even catches up. That singular, brutal clarity when you're the one who's supposed to make everything okay. And yes, the crash afterward is hell. But the high? There's nothing like it. And nothing that quite replaces it.

In a way, it's better than sex.

It's a sick romance — me and the job. Full of damage and devotion.

But I'm not on the rig anymore. I've traded sirens for silence, chaos for calm. And yet, those ghosts still whisper. They cling to me. Hide in the folds of my skin. They don't shout anymore, but they don't leave either.

So now, when the sirens come howling past, I don't reach for a bottle. I reach for something else.

The birds.

It sounds stupid, I know. But they help. I close my eyes, try to focus on their song instead of the mechanical wail echoing down the highway. I watch the grass move, tall and patient in the wind. I remind myself that I'm here. I'm not kneeling in blood. I'm not breaking ribs with every compression. I'm standing in a field, in a life that is mine. Still mine.

The death I've seen, the lives I've held and lost — they're part of me. They always will be. But they don't get to drive anymore. I've wrestled that wheel back.

PTSD, you bastard, you don't get to win.

I do.

I'm here. I'm alive. I'm not drinking. I'm listening. To birds, to wind, to life.

And in this moment, that's enough. I am enough.

# Tea, My Bitter Old Friend

There's something strangely therapeutic about stirring a cup of tea. The soft clink of the spoon against porcelain, the lazy whirlpool of milk meeting hot water, the way the swirl settles into something quiet and steady; like it knows the chaos was necessary. It's a moment. One of the few rituals in life that feels like it was invented to mend something invisible in us. But, if you've lived a life like mine, sometimes all it takes is a spoon to summon the ghosts.

I was twelve, maybe. Standing at the kitchen counter, spoon in hand, waiting for the kettle to hit its crescendo. This was ritual too — but not the calm, soul-soothing kind. No. This was the kind built on shaky ground, steeped in nerves. As a kid, my mother would call out for her tea the way royalty might request the execution of a traitor. Sharp. Certain. Impatient.

It should've been easy — a cup of tea. But nothing was ever just what it was with her. It wasn't water, bag, milk, sugar, stir. It was a test. One I failed regularly.

"What is this, bloody piss water? Make it again."

That one was a classic. So was: "God, you're useless. What good are you? Can't even make a bloody cuppa tea right."

She never stopped asking, though. That's the real curiosity. Never stopped sending me into the kitchen like it was some rite of passage I kept flunking.

And believe me, I wasn't trying to make it bad. I wasn't spiking her Earl Grey with contempt. I was just... a kid. Preoccupied with being anywhere else, doing anything else. Not out to sabotage the Queen's drink.

Thing is, those words? They stick. They crawl under the skin and set up shop. A slap bruises for a week. But that voice, those jabs? They echo. Long past childhood. Long past home.

They show up later: in the army, when I got something wrong, I'd call myself every name she used and invent new ones just to twist the knife a little deeper. As a medic, every time I lost someone, I didn't just grieve the death — I punished myself for it.

"If I can't make a cup of tea, what the hell made me think I could save a life?"

That's the math my brain did. Still does, some days.

You don't grow out of that kind of self-beratement. You don't wake up one day and decide you're enough. No. You fight for it. You stir and stir and hope the bitterness dissipates with time and sugar.

Sometimes, when I'm making tea now (still, to this day) I hear her. Not the full speech. Just a line here and there. Like a haunt. A glitch in the steam.

"You bloody idiot. Why don't you use your head for something other than a hat-rack?"

Charming, right?

So I sit with it. With the cup. With the past. Let the heat rise and fall, let the steam carry something old away with it. Not all of it — I'm not naïve. But enough. Enough to breathe. Enough to forgive. Enough to be here, now.

And the truth? The real truth I'm learning in the quiet? Life is kind of like tea. A balancing act. Too much of one thing and it's ruined. Not enough of another, and it's bland. You stir, you sip, you try again. Some cups are perfect. Some are barely drinkable. But they're all part of the process.

So here's to the imperfect ones. The ones that taught us something. The ones that burned our lips but reminded us we were still alive. Here's to the resilience of second tries.

And to my mother — may she rest — I hope she finally found a cup that's just right. Or maybe, more than that, I hope she found peace. Because I'm still learning how to brew my own.

# MORNING TEA & ROSC

Every morning, a man settles into his backyard chair, sipping tea beneath the elegance of a rising sun. Steam lifts from his cup like an early morning stretch. His white beard hums quietly of a life well lived. His quietude shows contentment for the moment. No rushing forward, no looking back.

From my back patio, I see this man, and I can't help but smile.

Some people spend their whole lives chasing paintings that make them feel something—brushstrokes from some fabled artist, given a price tag of astronomical proportion, sold to the highest bidder. And here I am: middle-aged and ordinary, living in some small town few have ever heard of, even fewer could find on a map—witnessing, in real time, one of the most peaceful sights to ever paint itself to life.

My neighbours, Rod and his lovely wife, Colleen, sit and enjoy their cuppa, woven in the other's company. It's a view most artists would fail to capture. But life—bless it—has granted me the quiet privilege of watching this real-life watercolour come to life each morning, just before the bustle of the day begins.

"Hey, Rod! Colleen," I chirp and wave.

"Oh, hello, Matthew," Rod returns. His timbre: gentle and low. A spoken cello of cordiality.

This couple, my beautiful neighbours, serve as a reminder that it's alright to pause and slow things down every now and again. Life can move pretty fast when it wants to.

In this spinning wheel we call life, there are few certainties—one of which is death. A notion we often pay little to no mind. Which is good. Because the sad irony is that if we dwelled on the inevitability of our own demise, we would rob ourselves of the opportunity to live.

But sometimes, as is also the case with many great paintings, a blemish exists. For the Mona Lisa, it's the smile. The smirk. The ambiguous mouth curl. A curious imperfection that has divided art enthusiasts for generations.

On the 29th of May, a blemish occurred among the sweeping grasslands of my little town. Rod suffered a heart attack. The serenity and humility of our surroundings stilled beneath an air of chaos and uncertainty.

Panicked knocks mimicked thunder on our front door. I was doing some writing at the time, but after hearing the rapping, I got up to see what was going on. Peering through the blinds, I saw Robbie—a woman from a neighbouring community who teaches at the school here in town.

She had been driving up the road, as she had done a thousand times before, on her way to pick up her son from his friend's place. As the sun began to fall for the night, Robbie noticed something out of place. In a small town like Falkland, everything has its place—and if even the smallest of things are askew, it's immediately noticeable to a keen eye.

She spotted Rod's truck, swallowed by the tall grass lining the ditch on the side of the road. Rod had been on his way somewhere when his larger-than-life heart suddenly fell silent.

By the time Robbie had come to my door, a small group of men and women—all neighbours of Rod's—had already rushed to see what they could do. I threw on my shoes and bolted out the door. Even before making it the dozen or so steps from my driveway, I could tell Rod was in real trouble.

As a paramedic, you develop a feel for the subtleties of the human condition—especially when it is unwell.

I'll spare the details of what Rod looked like. To me, that's not important for this story. What is important is that in a man's time of life-and-death need, neighbours came together as saviours. As family. Without question, the only priority became our dear friend, Rod.

As someone who lives with PTSD and a mind full of ghosts, I had often wondered what I'd do if such an emergency were to arise. I feared I'd freeze. Or forget what to do. But against all odds—and in protest of my wounded mind and heart—I fell back into medic form and began compressions on Rod's chest.

Collectively, we performed CPR, utilized a public access AED, and delivered one shock. And when paramedics arrived, we had achieved the impossible—ROSC. Return of Spontaneous Circulation. Rod's heart had found its way back to him. So had the air to his lungs.

I don't recall much about what happened after the paramedics arrived. My mind started bending time, folding me into places I once was. My knees felt like they had glass in them—an echo from other days when I knelt roadside, pressing on someone's chest. My dear Sheena tried her best to keep me grounded in the present.

I remember watching the ambulance turn around and grow smaller in the distance as it made its way to the highway. My eyes followed the flickering red and white lights until they disappeared over the horizon.

The next morning, when I stepped out to let the dogs run and partake in my usual routine, I looked to the left—where Rod should have been, sipping tea. But the space was empty, save for a tiny bird perched on the back of one of the chairs, using it as a launching point.

And though my own heart still beat with the rhythm of life, it ached with sadness at what I was seeing—or, perhaps more accurately, who I was not seeing.

I looked down at my hands and wondered if they had done enough. Or if my inability to stay fully present during the incident had let Rod—and the others—down.

For seven days, each trip to the backyard was a tentative one. I'd glance left, hoping against hope to see Rod and his beautiful wife, sipping tea and laughing about the cat going missing... again.

But for seven days, the chairs remained empty. The wind jostled the leaves and played among the grass, but everything felt lesser than it once had.

Then, on the morning of the ninth day, I was woken by the euphonous sound of Sheena's voice.

"Rod's home..."

I kicked off the covers, bounded down the stairs, and sprinted to the back door. The dogs be damned. I barreled outside, still squinting into the bright morning sun. Using my hand as a visor, I peered left.

And there—painted in all its magnificent glory—sat Rod and Colleen. Sipping their morning tea, embraced and backlit by the warm glow of the sun.

Perfection.

"Morning, Rod."

"Hey, Matthew..."

That simple return was one of the best sounds I have ever heard in my little life.

Rod—welcome home, my friend. This town, and each of its painted days, are so much more beautiful with you in it.

Enjoy your tea.

# You Knew What You Were Signing Up For

Every so often, when the topic of stress among paramedics comes up — and it does, because trauma isn't exactly a subtle houseguest; someone inevitably drops the all-too-familiar line:

"Well, you knew what you were signing up for."

Right. Like that's supposed to be some kind of mic drop. Like saying yes to a job meant signing away your humanity.

It always lands the same way — smug, dismissive, hollow. It's the conversational equivalent of stepping over a body and telling the guy holding pressure on a wound that he should've expected this. As if knowing the worst can happen somehow makes living through it easier. As if reading the words "death," "violence," or "trauma" in a textbook makes holding a dead kid feel any lighter.

Let me explain something.

Paramedics don't get into this gig for the glory. There's no glory. There's blood. There's heartbreak. There are the sounds people make when they realize someone they love isn't coming back. We step into chaos willingly, yes — but that doesn't mean it doesn't leave marks.

Saying "you chose this" is like telling a soldier the bombs shouldn't bother him... after all, he signed a contract. Sure, we train. We learn the protocols, memorize the rhythms, drill the techniques. But there's no simulation for what it feels like to hear a mother wail for her child. No classroom can prepare you for the dead weight of a body that just slipped away in your hands.

My older sibling, he used to say it all the time. "It's part of your job." And yeah, he's technically right. But so is bleeding, apparently. And yet we still rush to stop it when it happens.

Here's the part that gets me: we're not asking for sainthood. Just some understanding. Some support. A sliver of grace in the face of the unthinkable. Because despite the uniform, despite the badges and boots and bravado, we're still just people. People who witness things others couldn't bear to imagine. People who carry stories we can't tell at dinner parties. People who go home, kiss our kids, and try not to picture the ones we couldn't save.

PTSD isn't a weakness. It's not a malfunction. It's not proof we were never cut out for the job. It's proof we were. Proof we cared. Proof we showed up again and again until something inside cracked under the weight of all that caring.

And it's not just me. It's every medic who's ever stared too long at a ceiling fan in the dead of night, trying to forget the sound of someone's last breath. Every cop who replayed a shooting in his head while brushing his teeth. Every firefighter who still hears the screams when the sirens have long since gone quiet.

So yeah, we knew what we were signing up for. But that doesn't mean we don't bleed.

You want to help? Advocate for support. Demand better mental health care for first responders. Create space for them to talk — not just when they're breaking down, but before they get there. Remind them that asking for help doesn't mean they're broken. It means they're human.

Because that's what we are. Human.

And if that's not worth understanding, then maybe the problem isn't the job — it's the world that keeps asking us to do it, then punishes us for the bruises we bring back.

That hardly seems fair. Or am I wrong?

# Clarence, Let It Snow

It was Christmas, 1946, when the world first met George Bailey — a man slowly dissolving under the weight of his own story. He wasn't the festive archetype. No jolly belly laughs or glistening tinsel in the eyes. George was pale, tired, and so heavy with invisible burdens he might as well have had anchors in his shoes. That winter night, with snow falling in slow motion and the world seemingly asleep, George stood on a bridge staring down at the icy black below. He was trying to decide if the world would be better off without him in it.

It's a scene we all know. Or at least think we do.

Bailey had dreams once. Big ones. Travel the world. Build cities. Live a life bigger than Bedford Falls. But life — as it tends to — made other plans. The kind that arrive uninvited and refuse to leave. George felt like a failure. Not because he was, but because the life he imagined never materialized. And those missed dreams? They echoed louder than any Christmas carol.

But here's where things get weird and a little magical: an angel shows up. Not the glorious kind with wings and a booming voice. No, this one's named Clarence and he's... well, let's call him unconventional. But Clarence stops George. Saves him. And George, as we all find out, goes on to realize just how wonderful his life really is.

It's a Wonderful Life premiered December 20th, 1946. By all industry standards, it flopped. People weren't ready for it. Maybe the world needed more distance from the war before it could handle a movie about existential despair and redemption wrapped in tinsel. But like George Bailey himself, the film endured. It clawed its way into our homes, our hearts, and our traditions. Today, it's as essential to Christmas as regret is to a New Year's hangover.

But here's the part no one talks about at the holiday parties: It's a Wonderful Life wasn't just a movie. It was a confessional.

Because the man who played George Bailey? James Stewart — the Hollywood leading man with a voice that cracked like old vinyl and eyes that could see through you — had just come back from the war. And not the kind of war they write clean endings for. Stewart didn't play soldier in the studio lot. He flew B-24s over Germany. Twenty combat missions. Over 130 dead in one. Men he knew. Friends. Gone.

Stewart had rank, but no interest in privilege. He refused the easy road, chose to serve properly. And it broke him, or at least cracked something deep inside. He came back different. Quieter. Leaner. Shadows under his eyes, ghosts in his pockets. They called it being "flak happy" back then — what we now recognize as PTSD.

And then someone handed him a script. Said they wanted him to play a man on the edge. A guy who questions his entire existence. A man who wonders if it might've been better had he never been born. Timing, as they say, is everything.

What Stewart gave us on screen wasn't just acting. It was something rawer. Something unrehearsed. During the famous bridge scene, Stewart wasn't supposed to cry. But he did. Not for the camera. Not for the director. For himself. And when Capra yelled "cut," Stewart didn't stop. He stood there, broken and sobbing, while the crew looked on in silence. It wasn't performance. It was release.

Look closely at that film. There's a tremble in his hands. A darkness behind the smile. A fragility in the way he moves, like a man trying to hold it all together. And maybe that's why we believe George Bailey. Why the movie works. Because behind the character was a man who knew what it felt like to want out.

And yet... he stayed. Stewart stayed. Bailey stayed.

And we got a film that reminds us that maybe, just maybe, the world really is better with us in it — even if we don't always see it right away.

So every December, when that film flickers across a screen somewhere — when Clarence earns his wings and George hugs his kids like he's holding the universe together — I remember that the story on screen was only half the miracle. The other half was James Stewart himself. A man haunted by war, saved by fiction, and generous enough to let us see him bleed.

It is a wonderful life. Not because it's easy. Not because it's fair. But because sometimes, even when we're sure we've given all we have, we've still got something left — a scene, a second, a line delivered with trembling hands.

Here's to Stewart. To George. To staying.

It really is, a wonderful life.

# This is the End... For Now

Life can be many things. And yet, should I be asked to define it, I'd still stumble. Ask me back when I was injured and sick, and I'd have quoted Bukowski, Twain, maybe even Hemingway — something clever, cynical, or both. Ask me now, and you'll find me gushing. About how fortunate I am. About how lucky I've been in this strange little life of mine.

That's the curious thing about luck — like beauty, it only holds value in the eye of the beholder.

Think about it: luck means something different to everyone. Same with life. But there are common threads we use to stitch our stories together. Shared meaning. Shared ache. Shared awe.

This book is my story told in prose. A tapestry of moments — unpolished, nonlinear, sometimes wild, often uncoordinated — woven together until this very moment. This now. This present.

I don't know where life goes from here. A lot of unwritten chapters lie ahead. There will likely be more loss, more love, more sadness, more joy — because that's what life is. Not one grand narrative arc, but a kaleidoscope of moments. Of snapshots. Of truths we collect and carry.

We say we die only once — but I disagree.

Lose a parent to suicide, and tell me that isn't a kind of death. Lose yourself in addiction, and tell me you didn't feel something inside go quiet. In this life, we live and we die in moments. What matters is how we walk through the next one. Because that next moment — that's the one that can make us... or break us.

I've shared with you my trauma. My triumph. My Sisyphean struggles and my quieter redemption.

And now?

Now, I think I'll make a spot of tea. Sit outside in the backyard for a while. Maybe just breathe. Maybe wave to Rod.

# Afterword

Stay Connected

If something in these pages hit home, made you laugh, made you think, or just made you feel a little less alone, I'd love to hear from you.

You can find me here:

Website: www.authormheneghan.com

Whether you're a reader, a fellow first responder or veteran, someone navigating their own road through trauma, or just a human who wandered in with a cup of tea — you're welcome in my corner of the world.

Reach out. Say hello. Tell me what resonated. I actually read the messages.

— Matthew

www.ingramcontent.com/pod-product-compliance
Lightning Source LLC
LaVergne TN
LVHW091513200926
848483LV00008B/457/J
* 9 7 8 1 7 7 7 6 4 9 2 1 0 *